# Hudson River Lighthouses

## An Illustrated History

### Kevin Woyce

Photographs
by the Author

Kevin Woyce

# *Contents*

**The Hudson River**
*Photographed from the Vanderbilt Mansion National Historic Site in Hyde Park, NY*

## Chapter One

# *Stuyvesant*

THE HUDSON RIVER is more than 300 miles long. Only the lower half, from the falls at Troy to New York Bay, is navigable. This is the part of the river Henry Hudson explored in September 1609, and which he claimed for his employer: the Dutch East India Company.

On September 18, Hudson anchored his *Half Moon* near the eastern bank, twenty miles south of present-day Albany. Because the natives who greeted him brought a large number of curious children, his crew named the spot Kinderhoek, "Children's Corner."

Dutch settlers farmed the hills along the river. During the American Revolution, area farmers supplied much of the wheat that fed Washington's army.

An industrial revolution transformed the riverfront town of Kinderhook Landing in the early 1800s. Businessmen dammed Kinderhook Creek to power paper and textile mills. They baked clay from the riverbanks to make bricks, and when the river froze each winter, they cut the ice into blocks and stored it in insulated warehouses.

In 1823, the citizens of Kinderhook Landing renamed their town in honor of Peter Stuyvesant, the fourth (and last) Director-General of New Netherland. (Peter Minuit, who bought Manhattan from the Algonquin in 1626, was the first).

PETER STUYVESANT FIRST visited the New World in 1642, when the Dutch West India Company appointed him to run the colony on Curacao, the largest island in the Netherlands Antilles. Two years later, Stuyvesant lost his right leg while leading an attack on the Spanish-held island of Saint Martin. For the rest of his life, he wore a wooden peg in its place.

Stuyvesant came to New Amsterdam in May 1647. During his 17-year reign, he built the city's first schools and fortified the port against hostile natives and—more importantly—New England Yankees. The town's population quadrupled, from 2,000 to 8,000, but Stuyvesant was not well liked. Twice he ignored Company orders to return to the Netherlands. When village deputies brought him a list of complaints, he told them his authority came from "God and the Company, not from a few ignorant subjects."

By 1664, his "ignorant subjects" had had enough.

Earlier that year, King Charles II of England had given his brother James most of modern New York and New Jersey. Because Henry Hudson was English, the Crown conveniently ignored the fact that the navigator had claimed the territory for the Netherlands.

Four British warships sailed into the harbor in September. When their commander sent Stuyvesant a note demanding his surrender, the Director General tore it up and prepared to fight. But when he ordered his subjects to defend the town, most of them refused.

Peter Stuyvesant surrendered on September 9. Richard Nicholls, commander of the British fleet, took over as Royal Governor.

After spending a few years in the Netherlands, defending his decision to surrender, Stuyvesant returned to Manhattan. He lived the rest of his life on a 62-acre farm, or *Bowery*, north of town. New Amsterdam had become New York because the King's brother was the Duke of York. The North River is now the Hudson. But Stuyvesant's memory lives on. Wall Street is named for the palisade he built to defend the town, The Bowery for his farm, and Whitehall Street for his executive mansion.

PRESIDENT GEORGE WASHINGTON signed the bill creating the United States Lighthouse Establishment in August 1789. Part of the Treasury Department, the Establishment built the first Stuyvesant Lighthouse in 1829, a mile and a half north of Kinderhook Landing. One newspaper article described it as a two-story stone building, surrounded by a four-foot breakwater. But no pictures exist, and some sources say it was made of wood, not stone.

Volkert Whitbeck (or Witbeck) was appointed keeper in 1830. He lived in the lighthouse with his wife, Christina, and their daughters. On March 13, 1832, a family friend—a Mrs. Van Hoesen—visited the Whitbecks with her children.

The winter ice had begun breaking up, damming the river south of the lighthouse. Another neighbor—a Mr. Beecher—saw the water rise to the top of the breakwater. As he rowed out, the ice north of the light began to shift. Before he could convince the Whitbecks and their guests to leave, a wall of ice crushed the lighthouse. Beecher saved six lives that day, but two of Mrs. Van Hoesen's children died, along with the Whitbeck's teenaged daughters, Harriet and Elizabeth.

**Saugerties Lighthouse** is similar to 1868 Stuyvesant Lighthouse, which was demolished in 1933
*Photographed from the Ruth Reynolds Glunt Nature Preserve in Saugerties, NY*

Whitbeck returned to the station in 1835, when the government built a new stone lighthouse. Neighbors had petitioned the Treasury to continue paying his salary during construction. After he died in 1840, Christina Whitbeck tended the light for another dozen years. Her annual salary: $350. Their daughter Ann continued the tradition, keeping the light until 1866.

The Lighthouse Board—which replaced the Lighthouse Establishment in 1852—built a third Stuyvesant Lighthouse in 1868. The two-story brick building, similar to the 1869 lighthouse at Saugerties, stood on a new masonry pier south of the earlier lights. The white light was visible 11 miles away. Keeper Edward McAllister shared the lighthouse with several pets, including a dog and a parrot.

**Coast Guard icebreaker on the Hudson River**
*Photographed at Upper Landing Park, Poughkeepsie, NY*

**Left:**
Automated beacon near Stuyvesant, NY

The Board used the 1835 lighthouse for storage until it was "carried away" by an ice jam in March 1902. The ice also damaged the brick lighthouse, but the newer building was quickly repaired. It remained in service until 1933, when the Lighthouse Service replaced it with an automated beacon on a metal frame tower. After the government demolished the lighthouse in 1936, stone from the pier was used to build a porch for the Stuyvesant Post Office.

## Did you know…?

MARTIN VAN BUREN, the eighth president of the United States, was born near Stuyvesant in the village of Kinderhook. Elected in 1836, he was the first president born after the American colonies declared their independence. He is also the only president who did not speak English as a child; like most of their neighbors, his family spoke only Dutch. Blamed for the "Panic of 1837," a severe economic crisis, Van Buren lost the presidency to William Henry Harrison in 1840 and the Democratic nomination to James Polk in 1844. He tried one last time in 1848, as a third-party candidate.

During his presidency, Van Buren spoke so often of his hometown that associates called him "Old Kinderhook." Amused by this nickname, he began signing notes "OK."

Van Buren spent his last years at Lindenwald, his country estate near Kinderhook. The National Park Service maintains the house as a National Historic Landmark.

### Visitors' Information:
**Martin Van Buren National Historic Site**
nps.gov/mava/index.htm

## Chapter Two

# *Coxsackie*

JONAS BRONCK, THE son of a Swedish preacher, sailed on merchant ships to India and Japan before moving to New Netherland in 1639. He settled on the east bank of the Harlem River, across from the highlands of northern Manhattan. Neighbors called his 500-acre farm "Bronck's Land" and the river that flowed through it "Bronck's River." His property was divided after he was killed by an Indian war party, but the river still bore his name. English mapmakers labeled it the "Bronx River." In 1898, The Bronx became one of the five boroughs of the City of Greater New York.

Pieter Bronck, variously identified as Jonas's son, cousin, or younger brother, arrived in 1652. He built a tavern and brewery in Beverwyck (modern Albany), and then bought a stretch of riverfront the Catskill Indians called *Koixhackung*. (One possible translation: "Place of Owls"). The land was on the west side of the Hudson, 20 miles south of Beverwyck. The one-room farmhouse he built in 1663 is still standing, the oldest home in upstate New York. In 1939, Bronck's descendants gave the house to the Greene County Historical Society, which maintains it as a museum.

**Coxsackie, NY:** Industrial waterfront
*Early 20th century postcard*

Later settlers wrote the native name as Coxsackie (pronounced *Cook-sock-ee*). In 1775, when news of the fighting at Lexington and Concord reached the town, 225 citizens signed a short letter protesting "several arbitrary and oppressive Acts of the British Parliament." This "Coxsackie Declaration of Independence" may have been signed at the Bronck home.

Merchant Eliakim Reed built a dock and a warehouse on the riverbank in the late 1700s. Though he sold the property in 1804, Reed's Landing became a busy commercial district after the Erie Canal opened in 1825. When the West Shore Railroad arrived in 1880, Coxsackie was a thriving port with factories, shops, hotels, even an opera house. The steam ferry *Coxsackie* carried passengers, horse-drawn wagons, and eventually automobiles across to Newton's Hook in Stuyvesant.

**Coxsackie Lighthouse**
*Early 20th century postcard*

THE HUDSON IS narrower at Coxsackie than at any other point south of Albany. It is also divided by two small islands: Coxsackie and Rattlesnake.

The first Coxsackie Lighthouse, built in 1830, stood more than a mile and a half north of town, at the north end of Rattlesnake Island. Jonas Parker was appointed keeper in 1849, for an annual salary of $300; little else is known of the light's early history.

In 1854, the Lighthouse Board replaced the lantern's outdated apparatus—multiple oil lamps and metal reflectors—with an imported Fresnel lens. Invented by French scientist Augustin Jean Fresnel in the 1820s, Fresnel lenses use rows of prisms to focus the light of a single lamp. Light from the largest type, called "first order" lenses, can be seen up to 25 miles away. Coxsackie had a sixth order lens, the smallest made for lighthouses.

13

**Fresnel lighthouse lens**
*Photographed at the Sodus Bay Lighthouse Museum in Sodus Point, NY*

The Board built a new, red-brick keeper's house on a stone pier in 1868. The square brick tower attached to the northwest corner was just 32 feet high. William Hoose, who began tending the light in the 1850s, moved to the new building with his wife, Christina, and their children, Frank and Emma. The government transferred the small lens from the old lighthouse.

In 1872, Hoose received quarterly payments of $140, an annual salary of $560. He tended Coxsackie Light for 32 years. His son Frank, who took over in the 1880s, stayed on for another 18.

The 1902 ice jam that destroyed the 1835 Stuyvesant lighthouse also pummeled Coxsackie. Ice broke through the north wall, flooded the first floor, and crushed or swept away several smaller buildings.

ALONG WITH LIGHTHOUSES, the Hudson used to be dotted with dozens of smaller beacons. Most of these were just lanterns on wooden posts. Many were tended by part-time "lamplighters."

Coxsackie keeper Jerome McDougall maintained the East Flats Beacon, marking the shallows a mile and a half south of the lighthouse. On December 13, 1922 he climbed the wooden frame to refill the oil supply. The structure collapsed, plunging him into the icy water and tipping his boat. Unable to swim in his heavy winter clothing, McDougall pulled himself onto the boat.

A tugboat captain, who had been looking for the beacon, spotted McDougall. He released the scows he was towing, steered as close as he could to the keeper's boat, and tossed out a lifeline. Herbert Hoover, then Secretary of Commerce, wrote to McDougall in January, thanking him for his "heroic effort to maintain this light ... which will be noted on the records as part of your official history."

The *New York Times* profiled "Mac" that June, describing his daily trips to shore, the dance parties he hosted on the lighthouse porch, and his leadership of the local Boy Scout troupe.

By the 1930s, Reed's Landing was largely abandoned. When the steam freighter *Storm King* sank at her dock in 1938, her owners removed the engine and left the wooden hull to rot. Half a century later, her ribs could still be seen at low tide.

The Coast Guard demolished the Coxsackie station in 1940, replacing it with an automated beacon on a steel frame tower. On shore, Riverside Park has replaced the old factories and warehouses. But visitors can still catch a glimpse of the nineteenth century in the small Reed Street Historic District: 30 preserved commercial buildings, two or three stories high with ground floor shops and restaurants.

## Visitors' Information:

### Sodus Bay Lighthouse Museum
sodusbaylighthouse.org

## Chapter Three
# *Four Mile Point*

ON MOONLESS NIGHTS, or when fog hung low over the Hudson, river pilots estimated their distance from shore by firing a gun and waiting for the echo. This was done so often near Coxsackie that sailors named a bluff four miles south of town "Echo Hill."

The government built a stone lighthouse on top of the bluff in 1831. The lantern held seven oil lamps fitted with metal reflectors. The tower did not have an attached keeper's house. Instead, the Lighthouse Establishment bought and repaired a nearby stone house, which a retired sea captain had built several decades earlier.

In 1850, the Establishment recognized William Van Vleet for having the "best kept establishment on the river." Annual salary: $350.

When the Civil War broke out, Moses Walters enlisted in the Union Army. So did his father, and his three brothers. Only two of them survived: Moses, who lost a leg at Gettysburg, and one of his brothers. By 1869, Moses Walters was tending the Four Mile Point Lighthouse. He remained there until at least 1893, when he was making $500 a year. The Lighthouse Board replaced the stone tower in 1880, with one made of cast iron.

**Four Mile Point Lighthouse**
*Early 20th century postcard*

Like Coxsackie, Four Mile Point used to have an industrial waterfront. Ice warehouses lined the riverbank. But by 1928, traffic had dwindled. The Lighthouse Service removed the iron tower and replaced it with an automated beacon closer to the water.

The Scenic Hudson Land Trust bought the ice company's long-abandoned property in 1992, saving it from residential development. Now called Four Mile Point Landing, the 7.6-acre park includes walking trails, a pond, and river access for kayaks and canoes. The government sold the lighthouse property in 1931, but you can still imagine the view from the tower if you climb the short, steep trail to the observation deck.

The keeper's house still exists but is privately owned.

## Visitors' Information:
### Four Mile Landing
scenichudson.org/parks/fourmilepoint

Chapter Four
# *Hudson-Athens*

BROTHERS SETH AND Thomas Jenkins discovered Claverack Landing in 1783. The small Dutch village, settled in 1662, was on the east side of the Hudson, a hundred miles north of New Amsterdam. Its name probably came from the Dutch word for "clover."

Though the Revolution had ended, the British Navy was still harassing New England whalers. The Jenkins brothers had sailed up the river looking for an inland home for Nantucket's whaling fleet. Claverack's harbor, surrounded by high bluffs, seemed perfect. The surrounding property was also much cheaper than land closer to New York. In 1784, 30 Massachusetts and Rhode Island whalers arrived, with prefabricated houses stowed in the holds of their ships.

They were mostly Quakers, who had remained neutral during the war. Calling themselves "The Proprietors," they chartered the City of Hudson in 1785 and laid out a grid of wide streets. The parade ground they created on the edge of the bluff is now Promenade Park.

By 1790, Hudson was the eighth largest city in the United States. Shipyards and warehouses lined the riverfront. In 1797, Hudson missed becoming New York's state capital by just one vote.

The city owed its prosperity to the growing demand for whale oil. Before petroleum was discovered in Pennsylvania in the 1840s, whale oil was burned in lamps, including those in lighthouses. It was also used to make everything from candles and lubricants to shoe polish and perfumes.

Hudson City whaling ships sailed halfway around the world, on voyages lasting up to four years. They returned only when their holds were full. In 1789, the *American Hero* returned from the South Pacific with 2,000 barrels of whale oil. When the industry peaked in the 1830s, rival companies appeared in Newburgh and Poughkeepsie. The Newburgh company failed in 1837, the Poughkeepsie in 1843. The Hudson Whaling Company closed last, in 1845.

After the railroad arrived in the 1840s, Hudson became an industrial city of brickyards, breweries, cotton mills, and foundries. Today Hudson is known for arts and tourism; attractions include dozens of antique stores, a firefighting museum, and a restored 1855 Opera House.

FOR MOST OF its length, the Hudson is shallow and muddy. The shipping channel to Albany is kept open only with repeated dredging. In many places, sediments carried down from the Adirondacks collect to form "flats," just a few feet below the surface. Near Hudson, the Middle Ground Flats stretch almost two miles.

Henry Hudson ran aground on Middle Ground Flats in 1609. The *Half Moon* was not damaged, but he had to wait for the incoming tide to float it free.

**Half Moon replica**
*Photographed at Liberty State Park in Jersey City, NJ, in the mid-1990s*

Kevin Woyce

**Hudson-Athens Lighthouse**
*Photographed from Riverfront Park, Athens, NY*

By 1838, ship owners were asking the government to build a light at the south end of the flats. Congress finally appropriated $35,000 for a "Hudson City Lighthouse" in 1872. The following year, the Lighthouse Board built a square granite pier on pilings driven 50 feet into the riverbed. The north side is shaped like the prow of a ship, to deflect the ice jams that had battered earlier lights.

On top of the pier, the Board built a one-and-a-half story redbrick house, with a mansard roof and a square tower. Henry Best lit the lamp for the first time on November 1, 1874. When he died in 1893, his son Frank took over as keeper.

**Hudson-Athens Lighthouse**
*Photographed from Promenade Park, Hudson, NY*

In September 1905, Frank Best rowed to the tip of the Middle Ground Flats, where the passenger steamer *Young America* had collided with a larger ferry. Best and the ferry crew rescued several passengers and crew members, but four women drowned in the river. Seven years later, a steam tug struck the steamboat *Isabella* near the flats. Frank Best saved 11 women from the sinking boat and then helped tow it to shore.

Frank Best died in August 1918. His widow, Nellie, tended the light until a new keeper arrived in October. Frank and Nellie raised a son and a daughter at the lighthouse. To go to school in the winter, the children walked across the frozen river, or pulled themselves across the ice in a flat-bottomed boat. While Nellie Best tended the light in the summer of 1918, daughter Bertha rowed out in the station boat to rescue two people who had fallen into the river.

Emil Brunner came to the Hudson City Lighthouse in 1930. The kitchen was still the only heated room in the building. In 1937, Brunner rented a house on shore for his growing family (he and his wife had five children). Every afternoon, he rowed to the lighthouse. In Meade Schaeffer's cover painting for the December 28, 1946 *Saturday Evening Post*, Brunner is rowing to the lighthouse with his youngest son, Norman. The boat also contains a pile of wrapped gifts and a small Christmas tree.

The Lighthouse Board replaced the original lens in the 1920s, with a slightly larger one that rotated to produce a flashing light. The government finally installed central heating and indoor plumbing in 1938, electricity in the 1940s.

After the Coast Guard assumed control of America's lighthouses in 1939, most civilian keepers were allowed to remain at their stations until they retired, or until their lights were automated or deactivated. Brunner retired when the Hudson lighthouse was automated on November 10, 1949.

The station is now called Hudson-Athens Lighthouse. On the west side of the river, the Dutch settlement of Loonenburg became the Village of Athens in 1805. The larger Town of Athens incorporated ten years later. By 1900, Athens had three shipyards, four brick factories, and more than a dozen icehouses.

For more than a century, ferries crossed the river between Athens and Hudson. The first, launched in the 1830s, was driven by six horses walking on treadmills. From 1869 until 1921, steam ferry *George H. Power* connected the cities. Regular service ended with the retirement of the *Hudson-Athens* in 1947, a dozen years after the Rip Van Winkle Bridge opened, three miles to the south. In 2012, Hudson Cruises launched a new, hourly ferry service on summer weekends.

By the 1960s, the Coast Guard had plans to demolish five Hudson River lighthouses, including Hudson City. The Hudson River Valley Commission, founded by Governor Nelson Rockefeller in 1967, asked the Coast Guard to consider giving or leasing the historic buildings to nonprofits that could restore and maintain them.

Columbia and Greene County residents formed the Hudson-Athens Lighthouse Preservation Society in 1982. They began leasing the building from the Coast Guard two years later and acquired the title in 2000. Summers, the Society opens the lighthouse once every month for tours. There is a kitchen and a dining room on the first floor, four bedrooms upstairs. All have been restored to their 1930s appearance. The automated green light in the lantern flashes every 2.5 seconds.

Emil Brunner's first child, Emily, died in 2017, at the age of 92. In her later years, she sometimes gave tours of the lighthouse. She also recorded stories of her childhood there in the 1930s.

## Did you know...?

THE HUDSON-ATHENS Lighthouse has a twin sister in Long Island Sound: the 1877 Stepping Stones Lighthouse, visible from the Throgs Neck Bridge. Since 2014, the National Park Service has been working with the towns of North Hempstead and Great Neck to restore the building and to provide access. Like Hudson-Athens, Stepping Stones shows a flashing green light.

**Stepping Stones Lighthouse**, in Long Island Sound near North Hempstead, NY
*Early 20th century postcard*

THE UNITED STATES Treasury issued a "Hudson Half Dollar" in 1935, to commemorate the City of Hudson's 150th anniversary. The front is decorated with Henry Hudson's *Half Moon*, the back with the city seal: Neptune riding a whale. Because only 10,008 were made, uncirculated Hudsons now sell for more than a thousand dollars apiece.

## Visitors' Information:

### Lighthouse
hudsonathenslighthouse.org

### Opera House
hudsonhall.org

### Antique Stores
hudsonantiques.net

### Firefighting Museum
fasnyfiremuseum.com

### Hudson-Athens Ferry
hudsoncruises.com/group-cruises

## Chapter Five

# *Saugerties*

DUTCH SETTLERS WHO built a sawmill on Esopus Creek in 1677 called the waterway *Zagers Killetje*, "Sawyers Creek." By October 1777, when British warships anchored in the Hudson, the Dutch phrase had become "Saugerties."

The British had already burned the state capital at Kingston, along with the mansions of several prominent revolutionaries. Fortunately for the families living along Esopus Creek, the fleet's commander took his ships back to New York City when he learned of the American victory at Saratoga.

Entrepreneur Henry Barclay discovered Saugerties in 1825, shortly after the opening of the Erie Canal. Working with the Livingston family, Barclay bought land along Esopus Creek and built a dam, a paper mill, and an ironworks. By the time the West Shore Railroad arrived in 1883, Saugerties had a population of 4,000. Her mills produced eight tons of paper every day.

By 1934, Saugerties was a busy steamship port. Congress appropriated $5,000 for a lighthouse to guide captains past the shallows near the mouth of Esopus Creek. Local businessman Charles Hooster won the construction contract, with a low bid of $2,988.

The first Saugerties Lighthouse was a small wooden building with a short, round tower on the roof. The lantern contained five whale oil lamps, each equipped with a parabolic reflector. To support the house, Hooster built a stone-filled wooden crib measuring 40 feet by 50.

Abram Schoonmaker began tending the Saugerties light in 1845. When he died the following year, his widow, Dorcas, stayed on as keeper. The wooden building burned in 1848. Dorcas Schoonmaker survived the blaze—she lived until 1851—but she did not return to light keeping.

The government built a new wooden lighthouse in 1849. Joseph Burhans, who had tended the light earlier in the 1840s, was appointed keeper. He remained at the station until 1853. Christopher Reed was keeper in 1854, when the Lighthouse Board replaced the old array of lamps and reflectors with a sixth order Fresnel. The new lens made the light visible up to ten miles.

Dennis Crowley started working at the lighthouse in 1865. He stepped down just three months later, when he began losing his vision to cataracts. His son Daniel took over as keeper.

Congress approved $25,000 for a larger brick lighthouse in 1867. The Crowleys remained at the old station while the Lighthouse Board built a new granite pier, 12 feet high and 60 feet in diameter. On this they built an L-shaped, two-story house with an attached tower 45 feet high. After the Board transferred the lens to the new lantern in 1869, Daniel Crowley moved in with his parents and his younger sisters, Katie and Ellen.

The Board sold the old lighthouse for scrap, and then built a boathouse on the old pier. A short wooden bridge connected the two platforms.

Katie Crowley became keeper in 1873, when she turned 20. Besides keeping the light burning and helping her sister Ellen care for their parents—their father had gone completely blind—she made several daring rescues. In 1875, a young couple fell through the ice. Katie crossed the frozen river in a boat fitted with runners. To reach the woman, she had to dive through a crack in the ice. Two years later, Katie and Ellen rowed out in a storm to rescue the crew of an overturned sloop.

The last Crowley to tend Saugerties Lighthouse was Daniel's son James, who worked there from 1885 until 1895. Altogether, the family spent 30 years at the lights. Conrad Hawk was the station's longest serving keeper. Appointed in 1914, he remained on duty until a few weeks before he died in 1940.

By the time Edward Pastorini arrived in 1950, the lighthouse had electricity, steam heating, and even a telephone line. Before leaving four years later, when the Coast Guard automated the station, Pastorini repainted the three bedrooms on the second floor. The crew that closed the building removed everything of value and left the building to decay. By the 1970s, the Saugerties Lighthouse was in such bad shape that the Coast Guard had to move the lantern to a freestanding steel tower.

For several decades, Chester Glunt worked as a lighthouse inspector. His wife, Ruth, had traveled the river with him, getting to know the old lighthouses and the families that kept them. From their riverfront home, the Glunts saw the Saugerties Light falling into ruin.

**Saugerties Lighthouse**
*Photographed from the 1838 lighthouse pier*

Ruth Reynolds Glunt published an illustrated book, *Lighthouses & Legends of the Hudson*, in 1975. With architect Elise Barry, who advised the Hudson River Valley Commission, she then started a campaign to have Saugerties Lighthouse placed on the National Register of Historic Places. They succeeded in 1978.

The nonprofit Saugerties Lighthouse Conservancy bought the abandoned building in 1985. Total cost, one dollar. But after leveling the pier, they needed to replace all the floors, walls, and stairs, along with 10,000 crumbling bricks. They also built a replica lantern and relit the tower on August 4, 1990. The solar-powered LED lamp, focused by an antique Fresnel lens, dims every four seconds.

The picket fence surrounding the lighthouse is decorated with the names of hundreds of people who donated money for the restoration, plus all of the light's many keepers.

The Conservancy opened the lighthouse in the mid-1990s, as the Hudson Valley's most unusual bed and breakfast inn. There are two guestrooms on the second floor, a museum and gift shop on the first (exhibits include the station's original Fresnel lens). The innkeeper lives at the lighthouse year-round. He cooks breakfast for overnight guests and tells stories about the light's history. Guests who arrive by boat can tie up at the floating dock. A wooden bridge still connects the lighthouse property to the 1838 pier, which serves as the light's riverfront "back yard."

You can walk to the lighthouse from Saugerties, but check the local tide tables before setting out. The trail through the Ruth Reynolds Glunt Nature Preserve is half a mile long. At high tide, the section near the lighthouse may be underwater.

If you want to stay at the lighthouse, plan ahead. For popular weekends, you may need to book a year or more in advance. Visitors can also stay overnight at the Rose Island Lighthouse near Newport, Rhode Island; the Lighthouse Inn (formerly Bass River Lighthouse) in West Dennis, Massachusetts; and in the Race Point keeper's house at the northern tip of Cape Cod.

## Visitors' Information:
**Saugerties Lighthouse**
saugertieslighthouse.com
**Rose Island Lighthouse**
roseisland.org
**Lighthouse Inn**
lighthouseinn.com
**Race Point Lighthouse**
racepointlighthouse.org

**Race Point Lighthouse, Provincetown, Massachusetts**

**Lighthouse Inn, West Dennis, Massachusetts**

THE GOVERNMENT DECOMMISSIONED the 1855 Bass River Lighthouse in 1914, after the Cape Cod Canal opened. Businessman Henry Noyes bought the building at auction in 1917 and enlarged it for use as a summer home. State Senator Everett Stone converted it to a waterfront hotel in the late 1930s. On August 7, 1989—the 200th anniversary of the founding of the Lighthouse Service—Stone's descendants relit the lantern as "West Dennis Lighthouse."

RACE POINT LIGHTHOUSE is located outside Provincetown, about two miles north of the Municipal Airport. The American Lighthouse Foundation rents three bedrooms in the former keeper's house, two more in the nearby fog signal building. Only four-wheel-drive vehicles can manage the sandy "road" winding between the dunes of the Cape Cod National Seashore, from the airport to the lighthouse.

## Chapter Six

# *Steamships*

MACHINERY HAD ALWAYS fascinated Robert Fulton. When he was 14, he built a set of paddle wheels so he would not have to pull his fishing boat along with a pole. But as a young man, Fulton was more interested in art than inventing. At 17, he moved to Philadelphia to paint portraits.

Because the young nation offered so few opportunities for artists, wealthy clients advised Fulton to study in Europe. By 1786, he had saved enough money to visit England, where he met one of his boyhood heroes: Benjamin West, founder of the Royal Academy of Arts.

Like Fulton, West was born in rural Pennsylvania. He said the local Indians taught him to make paints by mixing bear grease and river clay. By the 1740s, Benjamin West had become one of Philadelphia's most popular portrait artists. Impressed by his work, Lancaster gunsmith William Henry commissioned a *Death of Socrates*, based on an old engraving. For West, it would be the first in a long series of historical paintings.

William Henry made guns for the British Army during the French and Indian Wars, and then armed the colonists during the Revolution. From 1784 until his death in 1786, he represented Pennsylvania in the Continental Congress.

In 1763, two years before Robert Fulton's birth, William Henry built and tested a paddlewheel steamboat on the Conestoga River. The boat sank, but Henry never lost his enthusiasm for the idea. He may even have discussed it with his inventive young neighbor. When Fulton was 12, he visited the gunsmith's home to admire his collection of Benjamin West paintings.

Robert Fulton was living in Paris in 1880, enjoying the success of his enormous historical painting *The Burning of Moscow*. Although this "panorama" is long gone, a nearby shopping arcade is still called *Passage des Panoramas*.

Fulton had not lost his inventive streak. While in England, he earned several patents. In 1801, he demonstrated an early submarine, the *Nautilus*, for Napoleon. The emperor passed on the opportunity to buy the "plunging boat" for his navy. But when Jules Verne published *Twenty Thousand Leagues Under the Sea* in 1870, he named Captain Nemo's submarine after Fulton's invention. The United States Navy also named the world's first nuclear-powered submarine *Nautilus* in 1954.

Encouraged by Robert Livingston, the United States Minister to France, Robert Fulton tested his first steamboat on the Seine in 1802.

LIVINGSTON WAS BORN into one of the wealthiest and most powerful families in colonial America. His grandfather—also named Robert—owned one of the four "manors" that covered most of modern New York State. In 1776, Livingston served on the Committee of Five that wrote the Declaration of Independence. The other members were Thomas Jefferson, John Adams, Benjamin Franklin, and Roger Sherman.

On April 30, 1789, Robert Livingston swore in George Washington as the first American president. As Thomas Jefferson's Minister to France, he negotiated the Louisiana Purchase with Napoleon.

Livingston first learned about steamboats from his brother-in-law, Colonel John Stevens. In April 1787, while attending the Constitutional Convention in Philadelphia, Stevens watched an unusual vessel churning along the Delaware River.

Built by clockmaker John Fitch, the steamboat was propelled by two rows of mechanical oars. By 1790, Fitch was ferrying 30 people at a time between Philadelphia and Burlington. Fitch patented his work in 1791, but never made a profit. His boats cost too much to build and operate.

In 1804, Stevens crossed from Hoboken to New York aboard the 86-foot steamboat *Little Juliana*, which he had named after his daughter. Decades ahead of its time, the boat was driven by twin screw propellers. Encouraged by this success, Stevens began building a larger passenger vessel, the *Phoenix*.

Livingston had convinced the New York State Legislature, back in 1798, to grant him a monopoly on Hudson River steamboat travel. When he returned from France, he formed a partnership with Robert Fulton.

On August 17, 1807, Fulton left Manhattan aboard the 130-foot *North River*. He docked at the Livingston estate, Clermont, 24 hours later. On his second day of travel, he steamed into Albany, 150 miles from New York. Fulton repaid Livingston by renaming the boat *Clermont*. By September, Fulton was running scheduled trips up and down the Hudson.

**Wooden model of Robert Fulton's *Clermont***
*Photographed at Trailside Museums in Bear Mountain State Park, NY*

Forbidden to operate *Phoenix* on the Hudson, Stevens put her to work on the Delaware, ferrying passengers between Philadelphia and Trenton. To get there, he took the boat down the New Jersey coast and around Cape May—the first steam-powered ocean voyage. His descendants opened the Stevens Institute of Technology in 1887.

Livingston died in 1813. Fulton succumbed to tuberculosis two years later. Their monopoly outlived them both. Daniel Webster, arguing on behalf of ferry operator Thomas Gibbons, convinced the United States Supreme Court to abolish it in 1824.

Top: **Hudson River Sloop**
Bottom: **Staten Island Ferry**

40

GIBBONS RAN HIS first steam ferry between two New Jersey cities: Elizabeth and New Brunswick. Eager to expand onto the Hudson River, he hired an ambitious young captain: Cornelius Vanderbilt. Under maritime law, the police could not impound a vessel unless they found the captain aboard. When they boarded Vanderbilt's boat, Cornelius hid in a closet until they left.

Vanderbilt had only taken the job to learn the steamboat business. He had left school at the age of 11 to help support his family and made his first fortune running a fleet of Hudson River sloops. When the Livingston monopoly ended, Vanderbilt left Gibbons to start his own line. He quickly crushed or absorbed his competitors, launched the Staten Island Ferry, and gave himself the rank of Commodore. In the 1860s, be bought and combined several unprofitable railroads to create the New York Central. When he died, his fortune was second only to John D. Rockefeller's.

In Hyde Park, visitors can tour a mansion built in 1899 by the Commodore's grandson. Frederick William Vanderbilt ran the New York Central for more than 60 years. Used for just two months in the autumn, this was the smallest of the family's Gilded Age mansions— "only" 54 rooms. Frederick Vanderbilt's niece, Margaret Van Alen, inherited the property when he died in 1938. She donated it to the National Park Service two years later.

BEFORE STEAMBOATS, THERE was little need for lighthouses on the Hudson. The most common vessels were Hudson River sloops, shallow draft sailboats steered with a long tiller. Most were less than 75 feet long. Pilots sailed with the tides, docked at night, and avoided foul feather and fog.

Because steamships could run against the tides, owners drove them all day and night, at speeds the old sloop captains never imagined. As the ships grew larger and faster, rival captains raced them along the river, sometimes with disastrous results. To keep them on course, the government installed dozens of lights on the river, both live-in lighthouses and the simpler post lights maintained by part-time "lamplighters."

## Did you know…?

ROBERT FULTON WAS not the only American inventor who started out as an artist. When Samuel Morse entered Yale at 14, he supported himself by painting portraits and miniatures. Like Fulton, he studied in England with Benjamin West. In 1840, he brought Louis Daguerre's photographic techniques to America, where he taught them to a young Matthew Brady.

Morse first imagined the telegraph—and Morse code—in 1832, while investigating electromagnetism. He sent the world's first telegraph message— "What hath God wrought"—on May 24, 1844. Visitors can see his art and inventions at Locust Grove, the Poughkeepsie mansion he bought in 1847.

## Visitors' Information:
### Vanderbilt Mansion National Historic Site
nps.gov/vama/index.htm
### Locust Grove
lgny.org
### Staten Island Ferry
siferry.com
### Hudson River Sloop *Clearwater*
clearwater.org

**Vanderbilt Mansion National Historic Site**
*Hyde Park, NY*

**Rondout II Lighthouse tower and lantern**
*Kingston, NY*

Chapter Seven

# *Kingston*

KINGSTON STARTED AS two Dutch villages, Wiltwyck and Rondout. Wiltwyck, founded in 1652, was a hillside farming community two miles west of the Hudson. The British changed its name to Kingston in 1664, after Peter Stuyvesant surrendered New Amsterdam.

Rondout took its name from a small Dutch fort, or "redoubt," built in 1614, where a creek flows into the Hudson. On old maps, the name is spelled *Ronduyt*. Because Rondout Creek was one of the best natural harbors in the Hudson Valley, the Dutch also built a trading post there.

The New York Provincial Congress moved to Kingston in February 1777, after the British seized control of New York City. Led by lawyer John Jay, the Congress drafted a State Constitution in April and held its first elections in June. George Clinton became New York's first governor on July 30. He held the job until 1795, and then again from 1801 to 1804. John Jay, who was Chief Justice of the United States from 1789 to 1795, served as governor from 1795 until 1801.

Kingston's time as State Capital did not last long. Warned that 30 British warships were sailing up from New York, the government fled in October 1777. On October 16, British troops burned all but one of the town's 116 houses, plus all of its shops and barns, the courthouse, the schools, and a church.

Kingston was quickly rebuilt. Rondout remained little more than a trading post until 1825, when the Erie Canal opened. That same year, brothers William and Marcus Wurts began building a second canal, to move anthracite coal from Pennsylvania mines to the Hudson River Valley.

Their canal opened in 1828. Though called the Delaware and Hudson (D&H), it actually ended at Rondout Creek. By 1872, when Kingston and Rondout joined to form the City of Kingston, Rondout was the busiest port between New York and Albany. Local businessmen soon ran out of warehouse space on shore and had to make an artificial island in the middle of the creek to handle the overflow.

John Bloomfield Jervis was chief engineer for the D&H. He began his canal-building career in 1817, as a 22-year-old laborer on the middle section of the Erie Canal. Trained as a surveyor, Jervis was quickly promoted to engineer.

After the D&H opened, Jervis worked for several railroads and designed the 44-mile Croton Aqueduct, which delivered fresh water from the Croton River to New York City. In the 1840s, he worked with architect James Renwick, Jr. on the High Bridge, which carried the pipes across the Harlem River to Manhattan. Renwick later designed Saint Patrick's Cathedral; the Smithsonian Castle in Washington, D.C.; and the brownstone lighthouse on Roosevelt Island, north of the Queensboro Bridge.

*Top:* **High Bridge (Croton Aqueduct)**
*Bottom:* **Roosevelt Island Lighthouse**

THE UNITED STATES Treasury built Kingston's first lighthouse in 1837, to help captains avoid mudflats at the mouth of Rondout Creek. The wooden building stood on a rectangular pier on the south side of the harbor entrance. The lantern on the roof held between four and seven oil lamps with metal reflectors (contemporary descriptions do not agree on the number). In 1855, the Lighthouse Board installed a sixth order Fresnel lens.

George Murdock moved into the lighthouse with his wife, Catherine, and their two children in May 1856. The building was decaying, and the pier had been damaged by shifting ice. The district engineer recommended the government enlarge the pier and add a triangular icebreaker with iron reinforcements, but it is unclear how much of this work was ever completed.

In July 1857, George Murdock was rowing supplies to the lighthouse when his boat capsized. Unable to swim, he drowned in the river. Though Catherine now had three young children to care for—one of them an infant—she kept the light burning until the river froze.

That winter, Catherine Murdock brought her family to Washington, D.C and asked to be appointed keeper of the Rondout Creek Lighthouse. The all-male Lighthouse Board—made up of naval officers, Army Corps engineers, and scientists—told her they did not employ female keepers. But she won them over with her knowledge and experience and returned to the Rondout Creek in the spring.

Catherine Murdock tended Kingston's lighthouses for the next 50 years.

Congress authorized the construction of a new, $22,000 lighthouse in 1866. The two-story bluestone building, completed the following year, stood on a round stone pier. Catherine moved in with her family after the

Lighthouse Board transferred the Fresnel from the old wooden tower.

When her children were young, Catherine rowed them to shore each morning during the school year, and then back to the lighthouse in the afternoon. On summer weekends, she gave tours of the station.

Shortly after the Murdocks moved to the new Rondout Lighthouse, the Army Corps of Engineers began building dikes to improve the harbor entrance. By the 1890s, these had changed the course of Rondout Creek so much that the lighthouse was of little use to pilots.

Catherine Murdock retired in 1907. Her son James, who had been appointed assistant keeper in 1880, was promoted to keeper. The following year, Congressman George Fairchild requested $30,000 for a new lighthouse, closer to the harbor entrance. He tried again two years later. In May 1911, Congress finally appropriated $40,000 for a new brick building. Construction began in 1913, just inside the north dike.

James Murdock lit the third Kingston lighthouse—usually called "Rondout II"—on August 25, 1915. The two-story brick house and attached tower stand on a concrete platform supported by wooden piles. The Lighthouse Service installed a fourth-order Fresnel, which showed a red light visible up to nine miles.

By the time James Murdock retired in 1923, he had spent 66 years at Kingston's lighthouses. During his tenure as keeper, he rescued a struggling swimmer, saved a man who fell off the dike into the creek, and helped raise a sunken boat. He even rowed to the aid of a seaplane pilot, who landed near the lighthouse because he was having problems with his engine.

**Rondout II Lighthouse, Kingston, NY**
*Hudson River view*

**Rondout II Lighthouse and breakwater, Kingston, NY**
*Photographed from Rondout Creek*

The Coast Guard electrified the station in the 1940s, and then automated it in 1954. For the next 40 years, the light was the responsibility of part-time "lamplighter" Warren Spinnenweber, who lived in nearby Port Ewen. He watched every night to make sure the light came on, and he inspected the building once a week. On foggy nights, he could turn on the fog signal from shore.

The Coast Guard removed the iron lantern from the old lighthouse in 1916 and tried twice to sell the bluestone building. After the roof collapsed in 1953, the government paid a local contractor to demolish it. All that remains is the stone pier, which looks like a small, overgrown island south of the harbor entrance.

Kevin Woyce

**1867 lighthouse pier**
*Photographed on Rondout Creek in Kingston, NY*

THOMAS CORNELL CAME to Kingston from White Plains in the 1830s. He owned three of the largest passenger steamers on the Kingston-New York circuit, including the *Mary Powell*—the "Queen of the Hudson." On the Rondout waterfront, he ran the Cornell Steamboat Company, which made canal boats, tugs, and river steamers.

Cornell also served two terms in Congress, helped start two banks and the Ulster & Delaware Railroad, and built the 481-room Grand Hotel in the Catskills. His successors opened the Kingston Point amusement park in 1896. Though the park closed in 1920, its carousel and dancehall once drew as many as a million visitors a year.

**Rondout Landing:** Preserved nineteenth-century commercial buildings in Kingston, NY

Unable to compete with the new railroads, the Delaware and Hudson Canal shut down in 1899. Cornell ended passenger service the following year, and many of Kingston's industries failed during the Depression. Several shipyards hung on through the Second World War, but when Cornell Steamboat closed in 1963, the Rondout waterfront became a ghost town. Over the next two decades, urban renewal projects and a new highway bridge destroyed much of the old business district. The remaining industrial buildings now house shops and restaurants. Parks, walking trails, and boat docks line the creek.

Kevin Woyce

THE HUDSON RIVER Maritime Museum, founded in 1980, occupies 385 feet of Rondout Creek waterfront. Artifacts, ship models, and paintings share the old boat shop with a research library specializing in Hudson River shipping and industries. Next to the building, visitors can see the *Mathilda*, a 72-foot steam tug built in Quebec in 1898.

The museum began leasing the Rondout II Lighthouse from the Coast Guard in 1984. Over the next four years, the interior was restored to its 1930s appearance. There is a dining room, a sitting room, and a kitchen and pantry on the first floor, three bedrooms and a bathroom on the second. Though the Coast Guard gave the lighthouse to the City of Kingston in 2002, the Museum still maintains it and runs the summertime boat tours. The Coast Guard operates the beacon: a solar-powered lamp that flashes every six seconds.

## Visitors' Information:
### Rondout II Lighthouse
hrmm.org/rondout-lighthouse.html
### Hudson River Cruises
hudsonrivercruises.com/sightseeing-cruises
### Kingston Waterfront
thekingstonwaterfront.com
### High Bridge
nycgovparks.org/park-features/Highbridge-park/planyc
### Roosevelt Island Lighthouse
rioc.ny.gov/179/The-Lighthouse
### Liberty Aviation Museum
libertyaviationmuseum.org

*Top:* **Steam Tug** *Mathilda*
*Bottom:* **Tug** *Gowanus Bay*, **Kingston waterfront**

**PT 728**

*Photographed summer 2008, outside the former Cornell Steamboat Company*

ALL BUT A DOZEN of the more than 800 wooden PT boats built during the Second World War were destroyed in battle or scrapped after the fighting ended. Like most of the survivors, PT 728 was launched during the last months of the war and never saw combat. She was brought to Kingston in the early 2000s by Robert Iannucci, a former Assistant District Attorney from Brooklyn, NY. Restored in the former Cornell Steamboat Company yard, she was relaunched as a tourist attraction on Rondout Creek in July 2008. Iannucci sold the boat in 2012, to the Liberty Aviation Museum in Port Clinton, Ohio.

**Kingston-Port Ewen Suspension Bridge (1921)**
*Rondout Creek, Kingston, NY*

**Esopus Meadows Lighthouse: tower and lantern**

## Chapter Eight

# *Esopus Meadows*

THE WEST SHORE town of Esopus, founded in 1811, took its name from an Algonquin phrase that meant "place of the small river." In this case, the "small river" was Rondout Creek, not the Esopus Creek that met the Hudson at Saugerties; Esopus was once part of Kingston.

The Esopus riverfront used to be lined with meadows. In the early 1800s, they flooded only at high tide. When the water was low, farmer George Terpening walked his cattle down from Port Ewen to graze. But the river was rising. By 1830, the meadow was a mudflat, mostly submerged even at low tide. As shipping increased on the river, so did the number of steamboats running aground at Esopus. Some of them had to be freed by tugboats.

Congress appropriated $3,000 for a lighthouse in March 1831. Six years later, the flats were still unmarked.

Stephen Pleasanton, Fifth Auditor of the United States Treasury, ran the Lighthouse Establishment from 1820 until 1852. Pleasanton had no nautical experience and little practical knowledge of lighthouses. As an administrator, he focused on keeping down costs. He always stayed within his budget, and some years he recorded a surplus. As a result, many American lighthouses were cheaply built, badly equipped, and poorly maintained.

But in 1837, Pleasanton had to ask Congress to *double* its appropriation for the Esopus Meadows Lighthouse. Because of its exposed location, he wrote that the building needed to stand "on a pier so strong as to resist the floating ice in the spring of the year."

Congress provided the additional money in July 1838. In August, the government bought the necessary land. According to some accounts, George Terpening sold the property for a dollar.

The bluestone lighthouse, completed in 1839, stood on a wooden pier with a triangular icebreaker facing north. Because wind and shifting tides often piled ice against the south side of the pier, the Lighthouse Board built a second icebreaker there in 1857.

A short octagonal tower rose from the center of the roof. Until 1854, when the Board installed a sixth order Fresnel, the lantern held four oil lamps with metal reflectors. Between 1839 and 1870, the Esopus Lighthouse had at least ten different keepers. Jeremiah Teerpenning was the first, spending three years at the station.

The station was showing its age by the time Jonathan Cole arrived in 1870. The Lighthouse Board had recently declared the keeper's house "unfit for occupancy in winter, even if the foundation pier were safe enough to justify its occupancy." In July, Congress approved the Board's request for $25,000 to build a new lighthouse on a larger pier.

The Board drove 250 pilings the following spring, 100 feet south of the existing light. These support a round granite pier 16 feet high and 45 feet in diameter. In the center stands a wood-frame lighthouse with white clapboard siding and a red mansard roof.

Jonathan Cole moved into the new lighthouse in August. 1872. The lantern held a new fifth order Fresnel, slightly larger than the one in the old tower, and visible up to 12 miles. The Lighthouse Board demolished the old building in 1873, but left part of its pier standing in the river. Cole remained at the station until 1885.

Like most of the Hudson lights, Esopus Meadows could be a lonely place to work. Keeper Andrew McLintock complained in December 1929 that for two weeks, foul weather and shifting ice kept him from going into Kingston for fresh food. John Kerr, who tended the light for the Coast Guard from 1944 until 1959, shared the station with his dog, two deodorized skunks, and a rooster. When he rowed ashore, the rooster sat in the front of his boat.

In the 1960s, the Coast Guard assigned three men to the station. They worked six days on, three days off, so there were always two on duty. When the government automated the light in August 1965, a *New York Times* reporter interviewed the departing keepers. The lives they described were not much different than those of their civilian predecessors: pulling groceries across the ice on a sled in the winter, rowing ashore in the summertime to collect their mail.

Within a year, the Coast Guard moved the electric beacon to a steel frame tower. The Hudson River Valley Commission blocked plans to demolish the building, but had a hard time finding anyone to restore or maintain it. In the early 1970s, several local colleges abandoned their plans to convert the lighthouse to a river research center.

**Esopus Meadows Lighthouse**
*Photographed from a sightseeing boat out of Kingston*

The foundation settled. Ice floes and barges crashed into the pier, cracking the stonework. By the 1980s, the east side of the lighthouse was sagging. The Commission covered the windows with boards and then painted curtains on them so the building would not look abandoned. From one, a painted black cat looked out at the river.

The nonprofit Save Esopus Lighthouse Commission leased the building from the Coast Guard in 1990. Successful fundraisers allowed them to stabilize the pier and re-shingle the roof.

Director Arline Fitzpatrick had a personal connection to the lighthouse. From 1937 until 1944, her uncle Manny Resendes was keeper. She often visited him at the station during summer breaks.

The Coast Guard gave the building to the Commission in September 2002. Stanley Fletcher, one of the Coast Guardsman who left the station in 1965, lit the new 250mm lamp on May 31, 2003.

When I saw the lighthouse in July 2008, from a sightseeing boat out of Kingston, a crew was repainting the exterior. Volunteers have since restored the inside as well. The Commission began offering occasional tours of the "Maid of the Meadows" in July 2010. There is a kitchen, a sitting room, and a dining room on the first floor; three bedrooms and a bathroom on the second.

Esopus Lighthouse is best seen from the water, or from the riverfront Esopus Meadows Preserve. It is also visible from some of the preserved estates on the east bank, including Wilderstein Preservation in Rhinebeck, and the Staatsburgh State Historic Site in Hyde Park.

HYDE PARK WAS originally Stoutenburgh, because New York farmer and merchant Jacobus Stoutenburg built a house there in 1741. John Bard, who was the first president of the New York Medical Society, inherited land nearby in 1764. Bard named his estate "Hyde Park" in honor of Edward Hyde, Royal Governor of New York and New Jersey from 1701 until 1708.

In the early 1800s, a local businessman called his store and tavern the Hyde Park Inn. Dr. Samuel Bard, who had inherited the estate from his father, was not amused. But the residents of Stoutenburgh renamed their town Hyde Park in 1812, after the tavern owner opened the area's first post office branch.

**Franklin D. Roosevelt Mid-Hudson Bridge**
*Photographed from Walkway Over the Hudson, in Poughkeepsie, NY (In this picture, and the one on page 65, both taken in March 2015, the Hudson is frozen)*

Claes van Rosevelt—the Dutch name meant "rose field"—settled in New Amsterdam around 1640. His farm occupied most of present-day Midtown Manhattan. By the 1700s, the name was spelled "Roosevelt" and the family had split into two branches: the Hyde Park and the Oyster Bay Roosevelts. Both produced a president; Theodore and Franklin were fifth cousins.

James Roosevelt bought a Hyde Park estate called Springwood in 1866. His only child was born there in 1882. Franklin Delano Roosevelt grew up at Springwood, returned there with Eleanor after they married in 1905, and used the estate as his "Summer White House."

**Walkway Over the Hudson**
(Formerly Poughkeepsie Railroad Bridge)
*Photographed from Mid-Hudson Bridge*

Roosevelt gave the estate to the National Park Service in 1943. The house is now a museum. His Presidential Library—the first of its kind—is located on the property, and he and Eleanor are buried in the Rose Garden. Val-Kill, the Hyde Park cottage where Eleanor Roosevelt lived from 1945 until 1962, is also maintained as a museum.

A few miles south of Hyde Park, the Mid-Hudson Bridge opened on August 25, 1930. Franklin Roosevelt attended the ceremony as governor of New York. The state renamed the span in 1994: Franklin D. Roosevelt Mid-Hudson Bridge. Its chief engineer, Ralph Modjeski, also designed the 1926 Benjamin Franklin Bridge (Philadelphia to Camden) and the 1936 San Francisco-Oakland Bay Bridge.

65

# Did you know...?

VERMONT ARCHITECT ALBERT Dow designed several wooden lighthouses, including Esopus Meadows and the 1870 Rose Island Lighthouse near Newport, Rhode Island. The Coast Guard deactivated the Rose Island Lighthouse in 1970; the nonprofit Rose Island Lighthouse Foundation began restoring it a decade later. The island can only be reached by boat, but the grounds are open daily during the summer. The Foundation sponsors occasional tours and rents the building's restored bedrooms. (Overnight guests are expected to spend part of their stay helping maintain the lighthouse and grounds.) Some visitors believe the ghost of Charles Curtis, who tended the light from 1887 until 1918, still wanders the house at night.

## Visitors' Information:
### Lighthouses
esopusmeadowslighthouse.org
roseisland.org
### FDR National Historic Site
nps.gov/hofr/index.htm
### Eleanor Roosevelt NHS
nps.gov/elro/index.htm
### Vanderbilt Mansion
nps.gov/vama/index.htm
### Wilderstein
wilderstein.org
### Staatsburgh
parks.ny.gov/historic-sites/25/details.aspx
### Walkway Over the Hudson
walkway.org

**Rose Island Lighthouse and Pell Bridge**
*Photographed from Newport, Rhode Island*

## Chapter Nine

# *Danskammer Point*

THE CORNELL STEAMBOAT Company had an unwritten rule: *do not travel in fog.*

Captain William Cornell had worked the Hudson for 30 years. On the evening of March 28, 1882, the fog was patchy at worst. Parts of the river were clear. He took the 310-foot. sidewheel steamer *Thomas Cornell* out of Marlborough at 8:20, heading south at what the *New York Times* called "a good rate of speed."

Three miles north of Newburgh, a rocky point of land stabbed from the western shoreline. There were no buildings or lights on the point. Neither pilot saw it.

A Dutch settler had named the point in 1663, when he saw Indians dancing there by firelight: "The Devil's Dance Chamber," *Duivel's Dans Kamer*. Two centuries later, the rocks were called Danskammer Point.

When the *Thomas Cornell* hit, her bow rode up onto the rocks. Her stern was left hanging over water 45 feet deep. When her frame cracked, the stern began sinking.

Amazingly, nobody was killed or even seriously injured. The crew took the women and children ashore with the ship's boats. The men climbed down a ladder to the rocks. Within 20 minutes, all 100 passengers were off the ship. When it began raining, the passengers huddled under stateroom blankets the crew draped over bare tree limbs.

Officers aboard *the John L. Hasbrouck*, steaming south from Poughkeepsie, spotted the wreck around 9:30 and picked up the passengers. Thirty disembarked at Newburgh, the rest stayed on to New York.

The *Thomas Cornell* had been completely rebuilt just three years earlier and was valued at $200,000. But the owners were only insured against fire. After salvaging as much of cargo and machinery as possible, they abandoned the shattered hull.

THE LIGHTHOUSE BOARD built a square wooden tower on the rocks in 1885. Standing 60 feet from the high-water mark, the lighthouse was only 31 feet tall. The ground floor was an oil storage room. Wooden stairs climbed to the lantern. A clockwork fog bell hung on the outside of the tower, 10 feet above the ground.

James Weist tended the light for 33 years, from 1886 until 1919. Because the tower was so small, he lived in town with his family. When he started at the lighthouse, he had to row out to the tower every afternoon. By the early 1900s, riverfront development had reshaped the shoreline so much that he could walk to work.

Lightning struck the lantern on July 11, 1914, paralyzing Weist on his right side. The next morning, he extinguished the light, crawled home, and called a doctor. Despite his injuries, Weist spent another five years at the lighthouse.

**Newburgh-Beacon Bridges**
*Photographed from Newburgh Landing*

In the early 1920s, the Lighthouse Service built a new frame tower on top of a small oil storage building. This light was discontinued by the end of the decade, and Central Hudson Gas & Electric built a coal-fired generating plant at Danskammer Point in 1951. After being badly damaged by Hurricane Sandy in 2012, the plant has been converted to burn natural gas.

ENGLISH SETTLERS FOUNDED the Parish of Newburgh in 1684, on land they bought from the Waoranek Indians. Gristmill owner Jonathan Hasbrouk built a one-story fieldstone house near the edge of the Parish in 1750. He enlarged the place 20 years later, and then rented it to the Continental Army in April 1782; George Washington made it his headquarters until August 1783. New York State bought the Hasbrouk House in 1850. Still run as a museum, it was the first American building preserved as a historic site.

**Mount Beacon and Hudson River**
*Photographed from Newburgh Landing*

Newburgh incorporated as a village in 1800 and then as a city in 1865. Thomas Edison supervised the construction of the city's first generating station in 1884. Shipbuilding was a major industry through the end of the First World War. In the 1930s, one of the nation's first Army Air Force bases opened just outside the city. The air base is now Stewart International Airport. The city's National Historic District, created in 1973, preserves more than 4,000 buildings dating back to the nineteenth and early twentieth centuries.

Across the river, Beacon took its name from the mountaintop signal fires that the patriots lit during the Revolution. Between the two cities, the Hudson is almost two miles wide.

For 220 years, the only way to cross "Newburgh Bay" was by ferry. Regular service began in 1743. During the Revolution, the boats served both sides. By 1910, there were three ferries in operation; 160 feet long and 35 wide, they each carried 30 automobiles. The last two ferries, *Orange* and *Dutchess*, were decommissioned on November 3, 1963—the day after the Newburgh-Beacon Bridge opened.

In planning since 1950, the bridge carried only one lane in each direction. A second, parallel span opened in 1980. The New York State Bridge Authority then closed the original bridge and began widening its roadway. Since 1984, the twins have carried six lanes of traffic, or about 20 million vehicles a year. To ease congestion, New York Waterway reestablished ferry service in 2005.

## Did you know...?

FOR MORE THAN 70 years, cable cars designed by the Otis Elevator Company carried passengers to the top of Mount Beacon, 1,500 feet above the riverbank. The summit boasted a casino and a 60-room hotel, until a 1927 fire consumed them both. Abandoned in 1978, the cable railway burned in the early 1980s. All that remains is a ruined powerhouse, at the top of a hiking trail in Hudson Highlands State Park.

OCEAN TIDES PUSH saltwater as far north as Newburgh, 60 miles above New York City. Beyond Newburgh, the Hudson is a freshwater river.

Surveyor Verplanck Colvin followed the Hudson to its source—Lake Tear of the Clouds—in 1872. The lake is in the Adirondacks, 4,343 feet above sea level on the side of Mount Marcy. Named after William Marcy, who was governor from 1833 until 1838, Mount Marcy is New York's highest peak: 5,344 feet. William Marcy later served as Secretary of War for President James K. Polk and Secretary of State for President Franklin Pierce.

## Visitors' Information:
### Washington's Headquarters
parks.ny.gov/historic-sites/17/details.aspx
### Hudson Highlands State Park
parks.ny.gov/parks/9/details.aspx

## Chapter Ten
# *West Point*

IN THE EARLY years of the American Revolution, the British tried to isolate New England by seizing control of the Hudson River Valley. Anticipating this strategy, Washington built a string of forts along the river. One of the most important was Fort Constitution, a gun battery on a low island on the east side of the Hudson, opposite the cliffs at West Point. To get around the Point and the island, ships have to make two right-angle turns, a quarter mile apart. Dutch pilots considered the passage so dangerous they called it Martyr's Reach.

British forces moved swiftly up the Hudson in October 1777. They took Fort Constitution on the seventh but did not stay long. After hearing about the American victory at Saratoga, Sir Henry Clinton turned his fleet around to protect New York. His troops abandoned Fort Constitution on October 20.

Washington's army rebuilt the fort, installed more batteries on the west bank, and stretched an iron chain from West Point to the island. To guard these works against land attacks, they also fortified the high bluff above West Point.

Designed by Polish military engineer Thaddeus Kosciuszko and named for one of the heroes of the Battle of

Saratoga, Fort Arnold was made entirely of wood and earth. The first guns were installed by March 1778.

But Benedict Arnold had grown disillusioned with the American cause. A proud man, he believed other officers had gotten credit and promotions that he deserved. Twice, George Washington had to talk him out of resigning.

Given command of West Point in August 1780, Arnold offered to surrender it to the British for 20,000 pounds. The plot fell apart in September, after American forces captured his coconspirator, Major John Andre, near Tarrytown. Though Andre was hanged as a British spy, Arnold managed to escape aboard the war sloop *Vulture*. Under his command, British troops captured Richmond, Virginia in January 1781 and burned New London, Connecticut that September.

At West Point, the upper defenses were renamed for Colonel James Clinton, whose troops had built them. The British never attacked them. After the war ended, the fort was converted to an ammunition depot.

John Adams first suggested creating a Military Academy in 1775. More than a quarter century passed before the first cadets arrived in 1802. Living in wooden barracks built during the Revolution, they studied military engineering, mathematics, and the French language.

THE NATURAL FEATURES that gave West Point its military advantages also made it a dangerous spot for sailors. Marshes join Constitution Island to the east bank of the river. Pilots have to steer west of the island, taking care not to wreck on the jagged shoreline below the West Point cliffs.

**West Point Lighthouse**
*Early 20th century postcard*

In 1853, the Lighthouse Board assembled a 32-foot frame tower at Gee's Point, the easternmost tip of West Point. (The point was named for Captain Cornelius Gee, who operated a fleet of Hudson River sloops in the late 1700s.) Keeper John Ellis lit the oil lamp for the first time on December 8. The Board moved the sixth order Fresnel in 1872, to a hexagonal wooden tower painted white with brown trim.

Sergeant Jeremiah Dinan kept the West Point Lighthouse shining for 18 years. Starting in 1888, he also had to wind the clockworks for the fog bell, which the Board had installed in a separate wooden tower closer to the water.

Dinan was born in Ireland in 1841. He enlisted in the United States Army in 1859 and remained at the lighthouse until shortly before his death in 1894.

Even with the lighthouse and the fog bell, West Point continued to trap the unwary. Strong winds drove the steam yacht *Idle Hour* onto the offshore rocks in October

1897. Two Academy cadets borrowed the light keeper's boat to rescue the passengers and crew. Two months later, the steamship *Emeline* grounded in thick fog.

The schooner *Philip Mehrhof* ran aground in 1921. The incoming tide shoved the boat into the fog signal tower, badly damaging the old wooden building.

The river's swift currents were especially dangerous for small boaters. In 1915, keeper A.P. Anderson rescued two boys from a drifting rowboat. Keeper Stephen Nolan saved two men in 1933, after their canoe overturned in a rainstorm.

The Coast Guard replaced the wooden lighthouse in 1946, with a flashing green light on a steel tower.

THE MILITARY ACADEMY grew slowly, gaining respect as its graduates proved themselves in the War of 1812, the Mexican War of the 1840s, and the American Civil War. Fears that West Point was creating a military aristocracy haunted the Academy into the 1820s, when Davy Crockett recommended shutting it down. Questions of loyalty surfaced again in 1861, when a lot of southern graduates resigned their U.S. Army commissions to fight for the Confederacy. Two of them were former superintendents: Robert E. Lee, and Pierre Beauregard. On April 12, 1861, Beauregard ordered the bombing of Fort Sumter.

To celebrate the Academy's hundredth anniversary in 1912, President Theodore Roosevelt personally handed out the diplomas. During this first century, there were never more than 400 cadets enrolled. Today there are more than 4,000. The Academy first admitted African Americans in 1870, but few enrolled until after the Army integrated during the Second World War. Women were denied entry until 1976.

## West Point Museum

West Point owes much of its modern appearance to Colonel Richard Delafield, superintendent from 1838 to 1841, and again from 1856 until 1861. Early in his first term, after reviewing competing plans, Delafield chose gray stone and Tudor-Gothic architecture for new barracks and academic buildings. With few exceptions, later planners followed his lead.

The West Point Museum is open every day except Thanksgiving, Christmas, and New Year's Day. Founded in 1854, it is the oldest museum run by the federal government. The collection moved to its current home, Olmsted Hall, in 1988. The Academy bought the building and grounds from Ladycliff College in 1980. Built in 1934, it was originally called Rosary Hall; Ladycliff was run by the Franciscan Sisters of Peekskill.

From April through October, the Museum runs ferry tours to Constitution Island. Visitors can also tour the Academy grounds. Sightseeing buses leave from the visitor's center, near the museum.

## Visitors' Information:
### West Point Museum
usma.edu/museum/SitePages/Home.aspx
### Constitution Island
constitutionisland.org

**Buffalo Lighthouse (1933)**
*Lighthouse Point Park, Buffalo, NY*

## Chapter Eleven

# *Erie Canal*

THE FIRST SHOT rang out in Buffalo at 10 a.m. on October 25, 1825. One after another, men stationed along the 363-mile Erie Canal and the lower Hudson River fired guns or small cannons, until the "report" reached New York at 11:15—the Erie Canal was open for business! Traveling at an average speed of four miles an hour, the boats that left Buffalo that morning reached New York on November 5.

The need for the canal had been growing for decades, as the United States expanded westward. Overland travel had always been slow, difficult, and expensive. When the Revolution ended in 1783, George Washington wrote that one of the nation's first priorities should be improving its roads.

Water routes had their limitations as well. A ship loaded anywhere on Lakes Erie, Michigan, Huron, or Superior had to be unloaded above Niagara Falls. The cargo was portaged around the falls and rapids to a second ship, which carried it along the southern shore of Lake Ontario to Oswego, and then down the Oswego River to Rome. There, the cargo was unloaded a second time, to be hauled six miles overland to the Mohawk River, which flowed into the Hudson. Two canal companies were chartered in 1792 to improve this route, but neither made much progress.

By 1812, talk of "improving" the route had given way to plans for an artificial waterway, flowing directly from Lake Erie to the Hudson. The project's backers included steamboat pioneers Robert Fulton and Robert Livingston, engineer James Geddes, and New York City Mayor DeWitt Clinton.

Fulton estimated that in 1811, he could ship a barrel of flour up the Hudson, from New York to Albany, for 25 cents. Driving the same barrel an equal distance over the state's primitive roads would cost two dollars. The Army soon proved him right, spending $2,000 to drag a $400 cannon from Washington, D.C. to Buffalo.

James Geddes worked as a schoolteacher before building a salt factory on Onondaga Lake, near Syracuse, New York, in 1794. Geddes began exploring possible canal routes for New York's Surveyor General in the early 1800s and was one of five engineers appointed to supervise the construction of the Erie Canal. The town of Geddes, near Syracuse, is named for him.

DeWitt Clinton began his political rise in 1790, as private secretary to his uncle George Clinton, first governor of New York State. Eight years later, DeWitt won a seat in the New York Legislature. He started the first of his three terms as Mayor of New York in 1803; during the third, 1811 to 1815, he also served as lieutenant governor and ran for president on an anti-war ticket. Incumbent James Madison won reelection by less than 8,000 votes.

By the time Clinton became governor in 1817, he had already convinced the legislature to fund several canal surveys and studies. Construction began on July 4, 181, in the city of Rome, which happens to sit at the geographical center of New York State.

The Erie Canal Navigation Company began manufacturing boats in February 1820. That spring, the middle section of the canal opened to shipping.

The entire canal—363 miles long, 40 feet wide, and four feet deep—was completed in eight years. Total cost, about seven million dollars. Although the governor's political enemies ridiculed "Clinton's Big Ditch," the Erie Canal was an immediate success. Because it opened in sections, there were already 2,000 boats on the canal in 1825. By opening day, the state had recovered the cost of construction.

Within 10 years, the Erie Canal was overcrowded. Dozens of companies were operating more than 3,000 boats. On busy days, 250 boats passed through each of the 83 stone locks.

New York began enlarging the canal in 1836, making it 70 feet wide and seven deep. All of the locks were rebuilt for larger boats, as was the 750-foot stone aqueduct that carried the canal over the Genesee River at Rochester.

By the 1840s, Erie Canal boats were carrying more than four million barrels of flour every year. Fifteen steam towboats worked the Hudson, each capable of pulling a string of 50 or 100 canal boats down the river to New York. Before the state stopped collecting tolls in 1883, the canal earned more than $121 million.

Like the great Hudson River steamboats, which carried a million passengers a year in the 1840s, the Erie Canal could not compete with the railroads that crossed the state in the second half of the nineteenth century.

**Erie Canal at Lockport, NY**
*1855 engraving*

Ironically, some of New York's first railroads were built in the 1830s to support the canal. Until 1851, they were allowed to carry freight only in the winter months, when the canal froze.

For nearly a century, teams of mules walked alongside the canal on a narrow "towpath." Each team pulled a single boat, at a steady four miles an hour. In 1918, New York rebuilt the canal again, this time for motorized vessels. Renamed the Erie Barge Canal, it remained a major route for oil tankers until the 1960s. Today it is used mostly by recreational boaters and sightseers.

## Visitors' Information:

### Buffalo Lighthouse

visitbuffaloniagara.com/businesses/buffalo-lighthouse

## Chapter Twelve
# *Stony Point*

KEEPER CORNELIUS LANSING lit the eight oil lamps in the Hudson River's first lighthouse on December 1, 1826. The short bluestone tower stood on top of Stony Point, a wooded peninsula jutting half a mile into the river from the west bank.

For northbound ships, the light marked the first major change in the river. South of Stony Point, the part of the Hudson called Haverstraw Bay is three miles across. North of the Point, a narrower Hudson winds through the mountainous Highlands.

ROBERT PARKINSON, APPOINTED keeper in 1829, had a family connection to Stony Point.

British troops took Stony Point from a small American force in May 1779. By summer, the redcoats had installed nine cannons, four mortars, and a howitzer behind sturdy earthworks. They also chopped down every tree on their "Little Gibraltar," so nobody could approach their lines unseen.

**Stony Point Lighthouse**

**Haverstraw Bay**
*Photographed from Stony Point Battlefield, NY*

In July 1779 George Washington sent the American Light Infantry, commanded by Brigadier General Anthony Wayne, to recapture Stony Point. Though Wayne's 1,200 men outnumbered the defenders two to one, he knew the British had all the advantages: high ground, artillery, even a gunboat on the river.

Water surrounded Stony Point on three sides, marshes on the fourth. The British had reinforced all the approaches with abates—lines of tree trunks sharpened to deadly points. The obstacles stretched out into the river, but not far enough to stop "Mad Anthony" and his Light Infantry.

**Hudson River Highlands and Bear Mountain Bridge**
*Photographed from the top of Bear Mountain, NY*

Wayne earned his nickname with daring plans most commanders wouldn't have tried. To even the odds, he launched his attack on July 15, at midnight. The tide was out, clouds covered the moon, and strong winds had driven the gunboat *Vulture* out of Haverstraw Bay. Wayne marched his troops around the exposed ends of the abatis and sent them silently up the hill, bayonets fixed to the ends of their unloaded muskets. In half an hour, the fort was theirs.

Wayne lost 15 men, but took 546 British prisoners, plus all of the fort's guns and supplies.

Though wounded in the charge, Infantryman Jacob Parkinson lived to pass the story down to his grandson, Robert.

IN 1838, A GOVERNMENT inspector reported that both the lighthouse tower and the nearby keeper's house were in poor shape. Both were repaired and updated in 1841.

Alexander Rose, appointed keeper in 1853, was married to Robert Parkinson's niece, Nancy. They had two young children, Alexander and Melinda.

The Lighthouse Board replaced the old lamps and reflectors with a fifth order Fresnel in 1856. Later that year, Rose collapsed while carrying wood down to the riverbank to build a fog bell tower. When he died a few weeks later, Nancy took over as keeper—a job she performed for the next 47 years.

The government demolished the riverfront fog signal in 1876, moving the bell to the outside of the tower. When the machinery broke down, Nancy Rose rang the bell with a hammer, once every 30 seconds. She once did this for 56 hours straight. But when reporters asked about her life, she told them, "Nothing ever happens up here."

Late one night in March, 1901, the steamship *Poughkeepsie* grounded near the lighthouse. When the passengers and crew—about 50 people—climbed up to the keeper's house, Nancy and her daughter Melinda made them coffee and sandwiches. In the morning, Nancy directed them to the nearest train station.

THE EMPIRE STATE Society of the Sons of the American Revolution joined forces with the newly incorporated American Scenic and Historic Preservation Society in 1895. Their goal: maintain the Stony Point Battlefield as a historic "reservation." After the state bought most of the peninsula in 1897, the Preservation Society worked with the War Department, the Lighthouse Board, and the town of Stony Point to open it to the public. In the 1890s, Stony

Point's town supervisor was Nancy's son Alexander, who did not share his parents' interest in lighthouse keeping.

Life changed at the lighthouse when the Society opened the Battlefield in July 1902. No longer isolated, the tower became a tourist attraction. Besides tending the main light, along with a smaller beacon the Lighthouse Board had set up on the riverbank in 1890, Nancy Rose had to play tour guide. She retired in 1903 and died the following year, at the age of 80. Melinda stayed on as keeper until 1905.

The Stony Point Lighthouse guided ships for 99 years. In 1925, the Lighthouse Service replaced it with a 29-foot frame tower on the riverbank. Without keepers, the old tower fell into ruin. Vandals broke down the door in the 1930s and stole the copper flooring.

The Palisades Interstate Park Commission assumed responsibility for Stony Point Battlefield in the early 1940s. To preserve the lighthouse, the Coast Guard gave the tower to the park in 1945.

As part of a 1995 restoration, the Commission installed an antique fourth order Fresnel and an automated, solar-powered lamp. When the tower is open for tours, visitors can climb the steep stairs to the second floor. The lantern can only be reached by ladder.

The wooden stairs outside the lighthouse descend to where the stone keeper's house used to be. The government replaced the original keeper's house, built at the same time as the tower, in 1880. The Lighthouse Service demolished the newer building in 1925, after deactivating the light.

**Stony Point Battlefield, main entrance**

Visitors' Information:
**Stony Point Battlefield**
parks.ny.gov/historic-sites/8/details.aspx
**Bear Mountain State Park**
parks.ny.gov/parks/13/details.aspx

Kevin Woyce

**The Hudson River frozen, with a shipping channel cleared by a Coast Guard icebreaker**
*Photographed at Poughkeepsie, NY*

## Chapter Thirteen
# *Rockland Lake*

FOR MORE THAN a century, ice harvesting was one of the Hudson River Valley's biggest industries. Every January, blocks of ice weighing up to 300 pounds were cut from nearby lakes. North of Newburgh, ice was even cut from the freshwater river itself. The blocks were stored for summer in big wooden warehouses, painted white to reflect sunlight. With sawdust packed between their double walls for insulation, these "icehouses" kept up to 80% of the blocks frozen. In the 1890s, the companies employed 20,000 men and shipped 2.5 million tons of ice to New York City every year.

Hook Mountain is on the west side of the Hudson, 25 miles north of the city. In the 1820s, several small companies set up there to cut ice from Rockland Lake. They combined in 1831, forming the Knickerbocker Ice Company. The name is a nod to Washington Irving, who had recently published a satirical *History of New York* as "Diedrich Knickerbocker."

**Icehouse foundations in Rockland Lake State Park**

Harvest time at Rockland Lake was late January or early February, when the ice was between 14 and 16 inches thick. At first the work was done entirely by hand. Later, steam-driven conveyors and elevators moved the blocks from the lakefront warehouses—the largest held 40,000 tons—to the riverfront docks. The company's own steamers and barges brought most of the ice to New York, but Knickerbocker also had buyers as far away as Australia and India.

The company's payroll swelled to 3,000 men in the 1880s. A small crew worked year-round, but most of the men were hired seasonally. In the warmer months, they tended their own farms, or took jobs at the nearby stone quarries.

**Southwest Ledge Lighthouse**
*Photographed from Lighthouse Point Park in New Haven, Connecticut*

THE LIGHTHOUSE BOARD introduced a new type of tower in 1876, at Philadelphia's American Centennial Exposition. Instead of wood, brick, or stone, it was made of cast iron. Designed mostly for offshore use, the factory-made towers could be shipped in pieces and assembled onsite from barges.

All that summer, a keeper lived in the Exposition's three-story tower. He lit the lamp every night, extinguished it in the morning, and then polished the lamp and the imported Fresnel lens. The Lighthouse Board took the tower apart after the Exposition closed in the fall, and then reassembled it on Ship John Shoal, in upper Delaware Bay.

Since 1877, an identical lighthouse has guarded the entrance to Connecticut's New Haven Harbor.

Instead of expensive wood or masonry piers, these new lights were built on "caissons." The caisson was a cast-iron tube, made in sections and then assembled in the hollow center of a mound of loose rock called "rip rap." The tube was filled with concrete to form a sturdy base, usually with a room-sized hollow in the center for storage or machinery.

The first two cast-iron lighthouses were octagonal, with the elaborate mansard roofs typical of Second Empire architecture. The Board adopted a simpler design in the 1880s: a plain conical tower, with a covered walkway around the first level. Twentieth-century sailors nicknamed them "sparkplug lights."

IN 1894, THE LIGHTHOUSE Board drove two rings of pilings into an oyster bed on the west side of the Hudson, near the Knickerbocker docks. On these, the Board assembled the caisson for the Rockland Lake Lighthouse. Because the pilings did not reach bedrock, the caisson settled unevenly. By 1920, one side of the "Leaning Tower of Rockland" was nine inches closer to the water than the other.

The government declared the lighthouse unsafe and replaced it in 1923, with an automated beacon on a 50-foot frame tower. Still in use, this light can be seen from the Haverstraw waterfront.

In silhouette, most caisson lights looked alike. The Lighthouse Board distinguished them in two ways: signatures and day marks. "Signature" refers to the light's nighttime characteristics, including color (usually white, sometimes red or green) and whether the light shines steadily or flashes. The automated beacon's signature is a white flash every six seconds.

Rockland Lighthouse, end of Palisades, Hudson River, N. Y.

**Rockland Lake Lighthouse**
*Early 20th century postcard*

Each lighthouse also had a particular color scheme, or "Day Mark." Ship John Shoal is red. The New Haven Southwest Ledge Light is white. The bottom part of the Rockland Lake Lighthouse was painted brown, the upper part white.

SHORTLY AFTER THE First World War, advances in refrigeration put an end to ice harvesting. Knickerbocker folded in 1924. The wooden warehouses were demolished two years later. All that remains are the stone foundations, a short walk from the lakeshore.

The Palisades Interstate Park Commission opened Rockland Lake State Park in 1958. The 1,133-acre park has a swimming pool and a playground, picnic areas, even tennis courts and an 18-hole golf course. The main trail around the lake is more than three miles long.

# Did you know...?

IN JANUARY 1912, a man named Robert Hopkins drove his automobile across the frozen Hudson from Tarrytown to the Rockland Lake Lighthouse. According to a short article in the *New York Times* (January 29, 1912), the river was crowded with "thousands of skaters," as well as people driving cars and riding horses along the frozen shoreline between White Plains and Ossining. The article does not mention what sort of car Hopkins drove, why he made the dangerous crossing, or what he did when he reached the lighthouse. (It also doesn't say when or how he got back to Tarrytown, though I assume he drove back over the ice.)

## Visitors' Information:
### Rockland Lake State Park
parks.ny.gov/parks/81/details.aspx
### Lighthouse Point Park
newhavenct.gov/gov/depts/parks/our_parks/lightho use_point.htm
### Harbor of Refuge & Delaware Breakwater Lighthouses
delawarebaylights.org

**Rockland Lake State Park**

# *Caisson Lighthouses*

Above:
**Robbins Reef Lighthouse, New York Bay**
*Photographed from Staten Island*

Top Right:
**Harbor of Refuge Lighthouse, Lewes, Delaware**
*Photographed from the Cape May-Lewes Ferry*

Bottom Right:
**Delaware Breakwater Lighthouse, Lewes**
*Photographed from the Cape May-Lewes Ferry*

## Chapter Fourteen
# Tarrytown

TARRYTOWN STARTED AS a Dutch village in the 1640s. The name probably refers the Dutch word for wheat, *tarwe*. Washington Irving offered a more amusing origin in his *History of New York*. He said Dutch housewives called the place "Tarry Town" because their husbands like to "loiter about the taverns on market days."

Irving also popularized the local nickname for North Tarrytown, with his 1820 story *The Legend of Sleepy Hollow*. In the story, schoolteacher Ichabod Crane tries to escape the Headless Horseman by fleeing to the Old Dutch Church. The Reformed Church of Tarrytown still uses the 1690s building on Christmas Eve, Easter Morning, and for summertime services

In 1996, the citizens of North Tarrytown voted to rename their village Sleepy Hollow. Driving up from Tarrytown on North Broadway (Route 9), there is a small park on the right, just south of the Pocantino River Bridge. The town installed an 18-foot, laser-cut steel statue of Ichabod and the Horseman in 2006.

**The Old Dutch Church in Sleepy Hollow, NY**

**Tarrytown, NY: Headless Horseman statue**
*Made by Milgo/Bufkin metal works in Brooklyn, NY*

Born in New York in 1783, Irving was named after George Washington. He moved to Sunnyside, his 10-acre Tarrytown estate, in 1835. During his last years, Irving wrote a five-volume biography of the first president, whom he met once in New York at the age of six.

John D. Rockefeller, Jr. bought Sunnyside in 1945. He opened it to the public two years later, restored to its 1850s appearance. Today it is one of four riverfront estates maintained by Historic Hudson Valley, the nonprofit Rockefeller founded in 1951 as Sleepy Hollow Restorations. The newest of the HHV sites is Kykuit, the home Rockefeller built for his parents in 1906.

**Washington Irving's "Sunnyside" in Tarrytown, NY**

THE DUTCH CALLED the broad stretch of the Hudson between Nyack and Tarrytown *Tappan Zee*. "Tappan" was the name of a local Indian Tribe, *Zee* the Dutch word for "sea." Half a mile off the eastern shore, shallows stretch from Tarrytown north to Ossining. At low tide, only two feet of water cover parts of these Tarrytown Shoals.

Congress authorized a lighthouse for the Shoals in 1847 and set aside $4,000 to build it. The Lighthouse Establishment considered several locations. One was Tarrytown Point, at the mouth of the Pocantino River. Another was Teller's Point, north of Ossining (or Sing Sing, as the town was called until 1901; residents changed the name to distinguish the town from the notorious prison). Teller's Point, now Croton Point Park, was covered with profitable vineyards and brick factories, so the owners were not interested in selling.

105

**Tarrytown Lighthouse and Tappan Zee Bridge**
*Photographed in 2008 from Kingsland Point Park, in Tarrytown, NY*

River pilots did not believe a light at Tarrytown Point would be of much use and suggested nearby Beekman Point instead. Owner Gerald Beekman felt that a lighthouse would spoil the river views from neighboring "country residences," but eventually offered to sell two acres for $3,000. The government passed.

The only remaining option—building an offshore lighthouse—would have cost much more than $4,000. In December 1848 Fifth Auditor Stephen Pleasanton wrote, "Nothing further ... has been done."

Ship owners and pilots continued petitioning for a beacon until 1881, when Congress appropriated $21,000 for an offshore caisson light. In 1882, the Lighthouse Board piled stone on the shallows, half a mile off Beekman Point (now Kingsland Point Park). The stone surrounded a cast-iron tube 20 feet high and 30 feet in diameter. This was partly filled with concrete, leaving room for a coal bin and a cistern. On top, the Board assembled a 48-foot iron tower, manufactured in Boston by the Smith Iron Works. The caisson is painted red, the tower white, and the lantern and railings black.

Jacob Ackerman, a retired schooner captain and former mayor of North Tarrytown, lit the oil lamp on October 1, 1883. Focused by a fourth order Fresnel—six feet tall, two feet in diameter—the light could be seen up to 13 miles.

Ackerman spent 21 years at the Tarrytown Lighthouse, retiring in 1904 at the age of 77. For company he had his wife, Henrietta, and all of their pets: a dog, three cats, and two dozen chickens. Sometimes one of the chickens walked off the edge of the pier, and Ackerman had to rescue it. He is also credited with saving the lives of 19 people.

**Tarrytown Lighthouse**
*Photographed from the riverfront Promenade at Edge-on-Hudson in Tarrytown, NY*

Tarrytown Lighthouse is five stories high. The lower three are lined with brick for insulation. The first floor is the largest, 18 feet in diameter. This was the station's kitchen and dining room. The second two floors, each about 15 feet around, were bedrooms. A total of eight windows lit these three floors. The fourth, used as storage space or an extra bedroom, had eight small portholes. The fifth and smallest floor, directly underneath the lantern, was the keeper's workspace, or "watch room." It also housed clockwork machinery for the 1,000-pound fog bell.

Most of the year, keepers could row to shore for supplies. In the winter, they walked across frozen river. But if the ice was unstable, getting to or from the lighthouse became almost impossible. On Christmas Day, 1898 the Ackermans invited local friends to the lighthouse to celebrate their 50th wedding anniversary. Shifting ice kept everyone home.

The Lighthouse Board installed a rotating Fresnel in 1902. From then on, Tarrytown showed a flashing red light. Winding the clockwork machinery for three minutes kept the lens turning all night.

The Coast Guard retired the tower's kerosene lamp in 1947, when the first electrical line was run out to the lighthouse from shore. Strangely, the government continued assigning families to the isolated station. In 1947, two young children who were living at the lighthouse drowned in the river.

By the time Richard Moreland moved in with his wife, Agnes, in 1955, the lighthouse had telephone service, forced air heat, and a propane stove. They even put a television on the second floor. But one night when the power failed, Richard had to hang a kerosene lamp in the lantern and ring the electric fog bell by hand.

A CBS camera crew visited the station in 1956, so Edward R. Murrow could interview the Morelands on live television. The show was called *Person to Person*. From a studio in New York, Murrow conducted two remote interviews each week. Richard Moreland said the hardest part of living in the tower was arranging furniture in the round rooms. His favorite part? No visits from traveling salesmen.

THE NEW YORK Thruway Authority began building a three-mile bridge across the Hudson in March 1952. Located less than a mile south of the lighthouse, the $81 million Tappan Zee Bridge opened on December 14, 1957. Because the eastern pier stands on the Tarrytown Shoal, the bridge was fitted with navigational beacons. The Coast Guard dimmed the Tarrytown Lighthouse in 1957, automated it in 1958, and then deactivated it in 1961. Richard Moreland retired from the Coast Guard to sell insurance.

By 1966, the government was planning to demolish the abandoned tower, along with the lights at Hudson, Saugerties, Kingston, and Esopus Meadows. The Hudson River Valley Commission convinced the Coast Guard to offer them instead to nonprofits or government agencies. In 1974, Westchester County acquired the Tarrytown Lighthouse from the General Services Administration.

The tower then was just 50 feet from shore.

*THE COSMOPOLITAN* WAS a family magazine in the 1890s. Editor and publisher John Brisben Walker ran articles on science, art, and travel alongside popular fiction and poetry. Fascinated by technology, Walker sponsored a "horseless carriage" race in May 1896: New York to Irvington and back, a distance of about 60 miles. Seven drivers started. Several dropped out with mechanical problems. One was involved in the city's first automobile accident (no fatalities, but the bicyclist he hit suffered a broken arm). Automobile manufacturer Frank Duryea completed the course first—in 7 hours, 13 minutes.

Around this same time, Walker began manufacturing steam-powered automobiles on the Tarrytown waterfront. The cars were designed by brothers Francis and Freelan Stanley, the factory by New York architect Stanford White.

The Maxwell-Briscoe Company bought the property in 1903, and then sold it to Chevrolet in 1914. Four years later, Chevrolet became part of General Motors, which began enlarging the factory in 1923. After the Coast Guard deactivated the lighthouse, the government allowed the automaker to build farther into the river on landfill.

IN THE 1970S, General Motors gave the Westchester County Department of Parks, Recreation, and Conservation permission to clear a pathway to the lighthouse. The County built a metal footbridge to the pier in 1979, and then reopened the tower for tours on October 1, 1983: the hundredth anniversary of its first lighting. In 2015, the County installed a plastic replica of the 1902 Fresnel lens, made by Artworks Florida.

The General Motors plant closed in 1996. In its place stands Edge-on-Hudson, 70 acres of apartments, retail space, and parklands. The riverfront "promenade" is more than a mile long.

In 2013, the Thruway Authority began building two cable-stayed bridges to replace the aging Tappan Zee. The westbound span opened in August 2017, and all traffic was diverted from the old bridge that October. When the second span is completed in 2018, the new bridges will carry a total of eight traffic lanes, four wide emergency shoulders, and a shared bicycle and pedestrian path with six scenic overlooks. The state began demolishing the 1955 bridge in May 2018. Much of the steel and concrete will be sunk off the Atlantic coast to form artificial reefs.

Officially the Governor Mario M. Cuomo Bridge, the new crossings cost just under $4 billion. The four concrete and steel towers are 419 feet high, and the roadway is supported by 192 cables—14 miles, in all. One of the towers will have a nesting box for peregrine falcons. Able to dive at up to 200 miles an hour, falcons were first brought to the Tappan Zee Bridge in the 1980s, to keep pigeons from nesting there—because pigeon droppings damage the paint that protects the steelwork.

The Village of Sleepy Hollow offers occasional tours of "The 1883 Lighthouse at Sleepy Hollow," which has been restored to its 1950s appearance. The tours begin at Kingsland Point Park. The tower can also be seen from the Edge-on-Hudson promenade, and will be visible from the overlooks on the new bridge.

## Visitors' Information:

**Tarrytown Lighthouse**
visitsleepyhollow.com/historic-sites/sleepy-hollow-lighthouse

**Sunnyside**
hudsonvalley.org/historic-sites/washington-irvings-sunnyside

**Kykuit**
hudsonvalley.org/historic-sites/kykuit-the-rockefeller-estate

**Old Dutch Church**
visitsleepyhollow.com/historic-sites/old-dutch-church

**Kingsland Point Park**
parks.westchestergov.com/kingsland-point-park

**Governor Mario M. Cuomo Bridge**
newnybridge.com

## Chapter Fifteen
# *Jeffrey's Hook*

IN 1762, MANHATTAN merchants held the first of two public lotteries to raise money for a New York Lighthouse. They built the tower two years later, at the north end of Sandy Hook. The original lighting apparatus consisted of 48 wicks floating in two large pans of oil, one suspended above the other. The Lighthouse Board installed the present third order Fresnel lens in 1857.

As traffic increased, the government built additional lights to guide ships into New York Harbor. The glow of the Twin Lights at Navesink could be seen up to 60 miles at sea. From 1823 until 1967, anchored lightships marked the main shipping channel. *Lightship Ambrose* (LV-87), now a museum ship at South Street Seaport, was anchored off Sandy Hook from 1908 until 1964. Staten Island's Fort Wadsworth Lighthouse guided ships through the Narrows until the 1960s, when the Verrazano Bridge opened. In New York Bay, several caisson lights warned pilots of shallows and reefs. Hurricane Sandy destroyed the bay's Old Orchard Shoal Lighthouse in October 2012.

**Sandy Hook Lighthouse and Fort Hancock**
*Gateway National Recreation Area, NJ*


Top Right:
**Lightship *Ambrose***
*Photographed at South Street Seaport, New York City*

Bottom Right:
**Fort Wadsworth Lighthouse and the Verrazano-Narrows Bridge**
*Photographed at Gateway National Recreation Area, Staten Island, NY*

**Statue of Liberty: the 1886 flame**
*Photographed in 2010, in the museum on Liberty Island*

Sculptor Frederick Bartholdi even designed the Statue of Liberty as a lighthouse. The light was supposed to shine through 25 windows in her crown. Shortly before her dedication in October 1886, the Lighthouse Board decided to put electric arc lights in in the torch's flame. Filtered through colored glass, 300 feet above the harbor, the light was often difficult to see. Bartholdi compared the flame to a glow-worm, and the Lighthouse Board relinquished control in 1902. Though the flame is still illuminated (now by floodlights), the statue has never again been listed as an aid to navigation.

NORTH OF BARNEGAT Inlet, offshore currents sweep sand north along the Jersey Shore. At Sandy Hook, this causes major erosion at the southern end of the peninsula, north of Sea Bright. The massive seawalls there were built to prevent the old Shrewsbury River Inlet from reopening and separating Sandy Hook from the rest of New Jersey.

These same currents continuously pile sand at the northern end of Sandy Hook. When the lighthouse was built, it stood 500 feet from the tip. Today the peninsula extends a mile and a half north of the tower. In 1817, the government built a small beacon to mark a sandbar west of the lighthouse. It was replaced in 1842, with two stone towers, each about 30 feet tall. Called the East and West Beacons, they looked like miniature copies of the main lighthouse. The Lighthouse Board fitted them with sixth order Fresnel lenses in the 1850s.

Neither still exists.

The Board replaced the East Beacon in 1880. The new 40-foot cast-iron tower had a flashing red light and a thousand-pound fog bell. Called "North Beacon," it was electrified in 1889. That same year, the government moved the West Beacon, 440 feet south and 250 feet west of its original beacon. Renamed "South Beacon," it was demolished sometime in the early 1900s. (The tower can still be seen in early photographs of Fort Hancock, which the Army built in the 1890s.)

Before the National Park Service opened Gateway National Recreation Area in the 1970s, most of Sandy Hook was used for military purposes. The Navy tested coastal defense guns on the long, empty beaches until 1919; the largest guns fired shells 16 inches in diameter. Fort Hancock, at the north end of the peninsula, protected the entrance to New York Harbor.

**National Lighthouse Museum**
*Former Staten Island Lighthouse Depot Foundry Building
(1912)*

The Army built new gun batteries at Sandy Hook in 1917, after the United States declared war on Germany. Because the North Beacon stood in the path of the guns, the Army asked for its removal. The Lighthouse Service disassembled the tower and moved it to the Staten Island Lighthouse Deport, next to the ferry docks.

The Lighthouse Board built the Depot in 1862, on the site of the old New York Marine Hospital, which had been used as a quarantine station from 1799 until the 1850s. Closed in 1965, the Depot fell into ruins. Of the original 18 buildings, only six remain. After more than a decade of planning, the National Lighthouse Museum opened in the Foundry Building on August 7, 2015. Future plans for "Lighthouse Point" include expanding the museum and adding residential and retail space.

JEFFREY'S HOOK WAS a small point of land on northwestern Manhattan, named for an eighteenth-century sloop captain. The Lighthouse Board marked the point in 1889, with a 10-candlepower lantern hung from a wooden post. A second lantern was added the following year. In 1895, the Board began asking Congress for money to build a real lighthouse; the first request was for just $3,000.

In 1896, New York City condemned five waterfront parcels, including Jeffrey's Hook. Working with the American Scenic and Historic Preservation Society, the city transformed the property into Fort Washington Park. Named for one of the two forts Washington's Army built in the summer of 1776 (the other was Fort Lee, across the river on top of the Palisades), the modern park stretches from 155th to Dyckman Street.

Fort Washington Park does not include the actual site of the fort. That's in Bennett Park, on Fort Washington Avenue between 183rd and 185th Streets. Located on Manhattan's highest ground, the park is named for *New York Herald* founder James Gordon Bennett, who bought the property in 1871. Every November, Bennett Park hosts a reenactment of the Battle of Fort Washington. By capturing the fort in November 1776, the British gained complete control of New York City. Washington abandoned Fort Lee a few days later and marked his army across New Jersey, to winter quarters in Pennsylvania.

The city gave the Lighthouse Board permission to build a lighthouse at Jeffrey's Hook, but Congress did not provide the necessary money until after the First World War. In December 1921, the Lighthouse Service brought the old Sandy Hook North Beacon up from Staten Island and reassembled it on the point.

**Jeffrey's Hook "Little Red Lighthouse" and the George Washington Bridge**
*Photographed in Fort Washington Park, NYC*

While the tower had been in storage, the Service replaced its windows with portholes and the original wooden door with iron.

There was no money for a keeper's house. Instead, the government paid William Knapp, superintendent of a nearby apartment building, to light the acetylene lamp every night and extinguish it in the morning. In foul weather, he switched on the tower's mechanical fog bell.

ENGINEER GUSTAV LINDENTHAL came to New York in 1884 with a dream: he wanted to bridge the Hudson River. He partnered with the Pennsylvania Railroad in the 1890s, to build a suspension bridge from 23rd Street to Hoboken. The project was put on hold after the economy crashed in 1893. Early in the new century, the railroad decided to build several tunnels instead of a bridge.

Lindenthal was appointed New York City Bridge Commissioner in 1902. Though he only held the job for two years, he supervised the completion of the 1903 Williamsburg Bridge and helped design the later Manhattan and Queensboro Bridges. The Pennsylvania Railroad hired him again in 1904, to design an arch bridge over Hell Gate, where Long Island Sound meets the East River. Now owned by Amtrak, the 1917 Hell Gate Bridge has a main span of 978 feet.

In the 1920s, Lindenthal lobbied the new Port Authority of New York and New Jersey to bridge the Hudson at 57th Street. His plans included skyscraper-sized terminals on both sides of the river; concrete and steel suspension towers 825 feet high; and a double-decked roadway 235 feet wide, carrying 16 railroad tracks plus auto lanes, light rail, and broad pedestrian "promenades."

**George Washington Bridge and Jeffrey's Hook Lighthouse**

The Port Authority chose a more economical design submitted by Othmar Amman, who had worked with Lindenthal on the Hell Gate Bridge. Amman was then supervising the construction of two bridges the Port Authority was building between Staten Island and New Jersey: the Goethals and the Outerbridge Crossing. He also designed the Authority's Bayonne Bridge, which opened on November 15, 1931.

The George Washington Bridge opened a few weeks earlier, on October 25, 1931. With a main span of 3,500 feet, it was the longest suspension bridge in the world. More than 55,000 vehicles and 35,000 pedestrians crossed it on opening day, 5.5 million in the first year. Though soon surprised in length by San Francisco's Golden Gate Bridge, which opened in 1937 with a main span of 4,200 feet, the GWB still holds the record for traffic lanes. It has eight on the upper deck and six on the lower. Together, they carry 300,000 vehicles every day.

The bridge's unique appearance is partly the result of budget cuts. Amman designed the 600-foot steel towers to be covered with granite panels. These were left off to shave a million dollars from the $59 million price tag. The Authority also scrapped its plans for grand plazas at each entrance, and nothing came of Amman's sketches for restaurants and observation decks on top of the towers.

The Port Authority also saved money by building at 178th Street, in Manhattan's Washington Heights neighborhood. With high ground on both sides—in New Jersey, the cables are anchored directly to the Palisades—the bridge did not need long approaches. (The Manhattan approach to the Williamsburg Bridge begins at Clinton Street, ten long blocks from the East River.)

IN THE 1930S, New York City Parks Commissioner Robert Moses embarked on his ambitious "West Side Improvement." This included enlarging the riverfront parks, relocating the New York Central Tracks, and building the Henry Hudson Parkway. David Barnard Steinman, another engineer who worked with Lindenthal at Hell Gate, designed the 1936 Henry Hudson Bridge. Supported by a broad steel arch, the bridge joins northern Manhattan to the Bronx. A second level was added in 1938.

Moses erased Jeffrey's Hook from city maps by straightening the shoreline with landfill. If he had his way—which he often did in the 1930s—the old lighthouse would be next. Bright lights on the George Washington Bridge made the little red tower unnecessary.

The Coast Guard kept the light shining until 1948. Three years later, the tower was for sale to the highest bidder—with the understanding that the buyer had 30 days to remove all traces of the lighthouse from Fort Washington Park.

The nation's children had a better idea: they wrote letters to the Parks Department, asking the city to help save their beloved "Little Red Lighthouse."

Hildegarde Hoyt Swift based *The Little Red Lighthouse and the Great Gray Bridge* on the tower at Jeffrey's Hook. Artist Lynd Ward sketched the bridge and the lighthouse onsite, and then finished the watercolor illustrations in his studio. A bestseller when it was published in 1942, the book has remained in print more than three quarters of a century.

Some of the children who loved the book sent nickels and dimes to support their cause. Robert Moses convinced the Coast Guard to cancel the auction and give the lighthouse to the city. But once the transfer was completed, the Parks Department neglected the tower for another 30 years.

By 1979, when the lighthouse was added to the National Register of Historic Places, it was rusting away. The Parks Department announced plans to restore the tower and the surrounding property in 1982. Three years later, *The Riverdale Press* editor Bernard Stein reminded readers of the Department's broken promise. The city finally repainted the tower, rebuilt its concrete foundation, and refurbished the grounds in the spring of 1986.

The New York Landmarks Conservancy repainted the lighthouse again in 2000, red with a white lantern. Two years later, the Parks Department and the Coast Guard relit the tower as a private aid to navigation. The modern 300mm lamp flashes once every three seconds.

Since 1992, the Parks Department runs an annual "Little Red Lighthouse Festival," usually in late September or early October. Highlights include local celebrities reading *The Little Red Lighthouse and the Great Gray Bridge*. More adventurous attendees can participate in the "Little Red Lighthouse Swim"—7.8 miles down the Manhattan shoreline, from the George Washington Bridge to Pier 62 at 23rd Street.

# Travel Tip:

THE LITTLE RED Lighthouse stands just south of the Manhattan tower of the George Washington Bridge, below 178th Street. It is possible to get to the lighthouse from 178th, but the path is not well marked. You're better off walking to the end of West 181st Street, where a pedestrian bridge crosses over the Henry Hudson Parkway to Fort Washington Park.

## Visitors' Information:

**Fort Washington Park**

nycgovparks.org/parks/fort-washington-park

**Sandy Hook Lighthouse**

nps.gov/gate/planyourvisit/sandy-hook-hours.htm

**Fort Wadsworth**

nps.gov/gate/learn/historyculture/fort-wadsworth.htm

**Navesink Twin Lights**

twinlightslighthouse.com

**Statue of Liberty**

nps.gov/stli/index.htm

**National Lighthouse Museum**

lighthousemuseum.org

**Lightship *Ambrose***

southstreetseaportmuseum.org/visit/street-of-ships/lightship-ambrose

**Bennett Park**

nycgovparks.org/parks/bennett-park

**Fort Lee Historic Park**

njpalisades.org/fortlee.html

Top Right:
**West 181st Street, Manhattan**

Bottom Right:
**George Washington Bridge and Palisades**
*Photographed from Fort Washington Park*

Kevin Woyce

**Titanic Memorial Lighthouse at South Street Seaport**

THIS 60-FOOT TOWER was dedicated on April 15, 1913, the one-year anniversary of the sinking of the Titanic. It originally stood on the roof of the Seaman's Church Institute of New York and New Jersey. Overlooking the East River at South Street, the lantern showed a steady green light. Every day, the globe was lowered precisely at noon. After the Institute moved to smaller quarters in 1968, the company that was hired to demolish the old building donated the lighthouse to the South Street Seaport Museum. It has stood in front of the Museum since 1976, at the intersection of Fulton and Pearl Streets. The light is longer operational, but a plaque on the tower still reminds visitors of its original purpose:

*"This lighthouse is a memorial to the passengers, officers and crew who died as heroes when the steamship Titanic sank after collision with an iceberg."*

**Lightship *Frying Pan***
*Photographed at Pier 66, Hudson River Park*

LIGHTSHIPS WERE ALWAYS named for the locations they marked. The *LV-115*, launched in 1929, spent 34 years anchored over North Carolina's Frying Pan Shoals. (On old nautical charts, the shoals were shaped like a round pan with a long handle.) After attempts to make a museum out of the ship failed (she sank twice at her dock), John Krevey bought the *Frying Pan* at auction for $8,000 and towed her to New York. She has been docked at Pier 66 in Hudson River Park since 2007, next to the retired fireboat *John J. Harvey*. In the summer, her decks are opened to diners as part of the Pier 66 Maritime Bar and Grill. (The pier is at the end of West 26th Street.)

*Frying Pan*'s rear mast broke off when she was salvaged in the 1980s, and has never been replaced

## H.W. Wilson Building, Bronx, NY

IN 1929, THE H.W. WILSON COMPANY—publisher of *The Reader's Guide to Periodical Literature* and other reference books—built an eight-story office building at 950 University Avenue in the Bronx. Because the company's logo included a lighthouse, the building is topped with a copper tower standing on a book. When a local storage company moved into the building in 2012, the new owners painted the tower orange. Though never an official aid to navigation, it is illuminated at night and can be seen from the Harlem River. Located northwest of Yankee Stadium, it is also a familiar landmark for drivers on the Major Deegan Expressway, the Harlem River Drive, and the Macombs Dam Bridge at 155th Street.

**Lighthouse Tender *Lilac***
*Photographed at Pier 25 in lower Manhattan*

THE LIGHTHOUSE SERVICE, and later the Coast Guard, used ships called "tenders" to deliver food, fuel, and other supplies to lighthouses. All of these ships were named after flowers or trees. The *Lilac*, launched in 1933, served Delaware River and Bay lighthouses until 1972. The nonprofit *Lilac* Preservation Project brought her to New York in 2003. Since 2011, she has been docked at Pier 25 in Hudson River Park (between Harrison and North Moore Streets). On summer weekends, Project volunteers open the ship for tours and other special events.

## Visitors' Information:
### Lighthouse Tender *Lilac*
lilacpreservationproject.org

## Selected Bibliography

Crackel, Theodore. West Point: A Bicentennial History. Lawrence: The University Press of Kansas, 2002.

Crompton, Samuel. The Ultimate Book of Lighthouses. San Diego: Thunder Bay Press, 2000.

DeWire, Elinor. Lighthouses of the Mid-Atlantic Coast. Stillwater: Voyageur Press, 2002.

Glunt, Ruth. Lighthouses and Legends of the Hudson. Monroe: Library Research Associates, 1975.

Holland, F. Ross. Great American Lighthouses. Washington, DC: The Preservation Press, 1994.

Jones, Ray. The Lighthouse Encyclopedia. Guilford: The Globe Pequot Press, 2004.

Levitt, Theresa. A Short Bright Flash. New York, W.W. Norton & Company, 2013.

Lewis, Tom. The Hudson: A History. New Haven: Yale University Press, 2005.

Shaw, Ronald. Erie Water West: A History of the Erie Canal 1792-1854. Lexington: The University of Kansas Press, 1966.

## Selected Online Resources:

New York Times archive
Lighthousefriends.com
Us-lighthouses.com
Hudsonlights.com
Lighthousedigest.com

## About the Author

KEVIN WOYCE is an author, photographer, and lecturer, specializing in regional American history. A lifelong resident of the Garden State, he grew up in East Rutherford—the eldest of fifteen siblings—and now lives in Lyndhurst. He speaks frequently, on a variety of historical topics, throughout New Jersey and southern New York State.

His books include:
*Jersey Shore History & Facts*
*Liberty: An Illustrated History*
*Niagara: The Falls and the River*

**Website:** KevinWoyce.com
**Facebook:** Kevin Woyce Author

Made in the USA
Middletown, DE
06 September 2021